Beads

Beads

An Exploration of Bead
Traditions Around the World

Janet Coles and Robert Budwig

Photography by Jonathan Lovekin

SIMON & SCHUSTER EDITIONS

We dedicate this book to beadmakers and beadlovers everywhere.

SIMON & SCHUSTER EDITIONS
Rockefeller Center
1230 Avenue of the Americas
New York, NY 10020

Text copyright © Janet Coles and Robert Budwig 1997
Design and photographs copyright © Ryland Peters & Small 1997

First published in Great Britain in 1997 by Ryland Peters & Small,

Simon & Schuster Editions and colophon are trademarks
of Simon & Schuster Inc.

Designed by Mark Latter

Manufactured in the United States of America

10 9 8 7 6 5 4 3 2 1

Library of Congress Cataloging-in-Publication Data is available

ISBN 0–684–83462–6

Contents

Introduction

This book will take you on a guided tour around the world of beads. It is by no means an exhaustive tour, but it is the story of many of the world's most interesting beads and the craftspeople who create them. Having visited many of the places where beads are made and talked to the beadmakers, we hope to inspire you to explore much further.

History of Beads

The great forces of nature terrified our ancient ancestors and it is thought that the first beads were worn as talismans to protect against such uncontrollable events.

Perhaps a convenient hole in a river-washed pebble made it easy to thread onto a piece of grass or leather and to carry around. Early manufactured beads were created using simple, readily available materials: bone, teeth, ivory, stones, seeds, wood, and a variety of plant and insect resins, all used to set off the daubs of clay painted on the body.

The earliest known beads, made of teeth and shells, were found in a cave in France where neanderthal people lived 38,000 years ago. Most of the world's earliest beads have disappeared and organic materials such as seeds and wood have long since decayed, but there are occasional finds of simple shapes in natural materials dating back some 10,000 years.

As the great civilizations of Egypt, the Indus Valley, Mesopotamia, and the Far East rose and fell, beadmaking flourished. Trade routes were established: from 6,000 B.C., Mediterranean coral was traded to the cities of Asia Minor, by 3,000 B.C., Afghan lapis traveled the 1,500 miles to Sumeria, and the Greeks of Mycenae traded bronze for Baltic amber.

The discovery of metal and glass produced technological advances that inspired a flowering of creativity. Exquisite handwork using these new materials proliferated. Techniques, especially for grinding and drilling stones, were developed using the bow drill, which still continues to be used today in some places.

The earliest forms of glass beads were found in Egyptian royal graves of the twenty-first century B.C., but a thousand years later, glass was commonplace and found buried in many tombs. Meanwhile, the people of ancient Crete were making remarkable advances in granulation, filigree, and repoussé techniques, and the ancient Chinese were making wondrous, delicate carvings in jade, a very hard stone.

As skills advanced and materials became refined, distinct methods of production were developed. It is astonishing that so many bead-making technologies appear to have been invented time and time again by different peoples in different eras. The tribes of the Caribbean coast of South America used rock crystal, drilling holes from each end to meet in the middle, simply using a stick dipped in quartz sand and rubbed between the hands to give friction—as did the Indians in Cambay. The bow drill was used by people as far apart as the Inuit of Baffin Island, the Highlanders of Papua New Guinea, and the Aztecs of Mexico, and continues to be used by some of the more purist of Native American beadmakers.

The lost-wax technique, used to cast finely detailed beads in gold, silver, and other metals, has arisen, apparently spontaneously, in cultures ranging from Pre-Columbian South America to Africa.

Eye beads, common in many parts of the world, were thought to protect the wearer from the baleful and covetous glance of the Evil Eye, a very strong belief among many peoples. It is thought that the eye bead will distract

Left Pre-Columbian (i.e. pre-1492) rock-crystal beads, made by the Tairona people from Colombia's Caribbean coast.
Right Early faience beads from Iran—forerunners of ancient Egyptian glass beads. Also shown is a necklace of shell and Neuva Cadiz blue glass beads, made in Venice and found in the archeological site at Neuva Cadiz in Venezuela.

the Evil Eye, thus dissipating its potency. Blue is a favored color for such beads, and they will often include a blue eye-symbol. Other amulets used against the Evil Eye are the cowrie shell and the hand of Fatima symbol.

Perhaps related in symbolism are the face beads of the Phoenicians and Romans, created in much the same way as millefiori beads, by layering individual canes of colored glass in the pattern of a human face.

The artistic impetus for beadmaking is often rooted in religion. Tibetans, for instance, made beads of turquoise, coral, amber, and—the most valued—dZi beads of agate etched with the mysterious patterns believed connected with Tibet's pre-Buddhist animist Bo religion.

Left Pumtek beads, from the state of Mizoram in northeast India, are made of opalized wood. The method of applying the patterns has always been something of a mystery. They are also highly prized by Burma's Chin people.
Right Neolithic banded agate and cornelian beads from Afghanistan.

growth in demand for beads had occurred when the Spanish conquistadores arrived in Central and South America. Much has been learned about our ancestors from archeological finds, and beads are present in the majority of excavations. Facts about trade routes, technological advances of materials and manufacturing methods, fashions, and habits can be learned from these finds, and it appears that we are constantly being surprised with new information.

Beads are increasing both in popularity and value. During the last 20 years more and more people have become fascinated by the history of beads, their significance, their collectibility, and their availability. Antique trade beads from Africa, nineteenth-century millefiori beads from Venice, pumtek beads from India and Myanmar (formerly Burma), dZi beads from Tibet, kiffa beads from Mauritania, chevrons, cowrie shells, Hudson Bay, and white hearts—are all part of a rich history to be explored and collected.

Contemporary Artist's Beads

Innovation in bead design and production techniques is ongoing. Contemporary beadmakers,

Below Old Venetian white heart glass beads.
Below right White heart beads are used in a Naga necklace from Nagaland, in the foothills of the Indian Himalaya. This multistrand necklace with its button-and-loop-style closure is typical of their work.

Above A string of Hindu prayer beads made of rudraksha nuts, sacred to the followers of Shiva, one of the Hindu trinity.
Top right Venetian chevron and melon trade beads produced for trade in Africa.
Below Used as a talisman against the Evil Eye, these Turkish eye beads are found all over Turkey, even embedded in footpaths.

Prayer beads are found all over the world (the word "bead" is from the Anglo-Saxon *bede*, "prayer"). They are crucial in the history of beads, helping sometimes-illiterate worshippers recite their prayers in the correct sequence prescribed by their faith. Visitors to the Middle East often see businessmen with "worry beads," a tasseled string of 33 beads, used for their steadying influence on decision-making.

Europeans made beads during the Middle Ages primarily for religious purposes. Rigid costume laws banned the wearing of jewelry other than the rosary, so a devotional need led to a burgeoning interest in beads. At this time, beads became known as *paternostri*, literally "Our Fathers," and Venetian beadmakers were known as *paternostreri*, forming elaborate and complicated guilds.

Great bead traditions gradually emerged. In Venice glassmaking skills, which for a period were solely a Venetian preserve, were directed into beadmaking. In turn, these skills were to travel north to Bohemia and west to the Netherlands. Later, these now well-established centers saw opportunities in the African market where slaves, gold, and ivory could be bartered for their beads. Two hundred years earlier a similar

especially in Europe and North America, are creating beads as fine as any of their predecessors. Their work could form the basis of an entire book, but it is impossible to single out the work of any one designer.

Collecting modern work can be an exciting occupation for the bead aficionado, and there are many talented craftspeople developing new techniques even today.

Finding and Buying Beads

Our hope in writing this book is that you will be fired with enthusiasm for beads and wish to create your own jewelry. Your first port of call should be your local bead shop—most large cities have at least one. There are also excellent mail-order catalogs available. Country fairs and street markets can be good sources, as can local yard sales and flea markets. Look out for broken jewelry—this may not be very expensive, and you can break it up and re-string it with other beads into your own design.

Probably the most adventurous way of adding to your bead collection, however, is to spend time during your travels exploring the local markets and shops. This can be a reason for choosing some of the more exotic parts of the world as your holiday destination—Africa, Eastern Europe, India, the Middle East, the Far East, and South America can be particularly rewarding in this way. Wherever you are,

you are sure to find exquisite examples of indigenous beadmaking traditions and you will also make some fascinating discoveries about ways of life that differ from your own.

It can take many years to accumulate enough knowledge to assess the provenance of a bead. If you are unsure of its authenticity, or if a bead is being offered to you at an inflated price, you should be wary. If, however, you know it is a copy but you still like it, and it is being offered to you at a reasonable price for what it is, buy it. Remember, too, that there is a whole category of "fakes" that have become valuable in their own right: early French glass replicas of jet, for instance, and other well-crafted glass beads, or early twentieth-century Bakelite plastic copies of amber are wonderfully decorative and are now very collectible.

We have chosen 30 projects to show some of the interesting ways of using beads in jewelry. However, we would urge you not always to follow the designs to the letter, but to use them as inspiration for your own creativity—after all, you won't always be able to find exactly the beads we have listed.

Top left Modern glass beads by Lucy Berganini of Weston, Vermont.
Above Modern silver beads, designed by British beadmaker Catherine Mannheim of Clerkenwell in London's East End.

Right These large blue-green disk-shaped lampwork glass beads, made by artist-beadmaker Karen Ovington of Evanston, Illinois, are interspersed with other smaller glass beads.

Europe and
the Middle East

English
Contemporary
Glass by
Patrick Stern

English
Contemporary
Wound Glass by
Heather Bellman

Whitby Faceted
Jet

German Wood

German Metalized
Plastic 'Silver'

Baltic Amber

NORWEGIAN SEA

NORWAY

SWEDEN

FINLAND

BALTIC SEA

ESTONIA

LATVIA

LITHUANIA

DENMARK

NETHER-
LANDS

GERMANY

BELGIUM

POLAND

Whitby

NORTH
SEA

IRELAND

UNITED
KINGDOM

London

RUSSIA

URALS

Contemporary
Czech Glass

Jablonek

CZECH REP.

Idar Oberstein

Paris

Neugablonsk
Kaufbeuren

FRANCE

RHINE

ALPS

RHÔNE

Lyon

Po

Venice

HUNGARY

UKRAINE

Turkish Silver with
Granulation

Turkish
Furnace
Wound Glass

French
Glazed
Ceramics

ITALY

Czech Glass
Rocailles
and Bugles

Greek
Ceramics

CAUCASUS

GEORGIA

BLACK SEA

CASPIAN SEA

Venetian
Glass with
Gold Foil

ADRIATIC
SEA

Naples

BOSPHORUS

TURKEY

SPAIN

PORTUGAL

GUADALQUIVIR

Venetian
Feather and
Swirl Glass

MEDITERRANEAN
SEA

GREECE

Iranian
Frit

TIGRIS

EUPHRATES

IRAN

SYRIA

IRAQ

Greek
Decal-glazed
Ceramics

ISRAEL

JORDAN

KUWAIT

PERSIAN GULF

BAHRAIN

Venetian
Blown Glass

Greek
Ceramics

Israeli Silver

Hebron
Furnace
Wound
Remelted Glass

UNITED ARAB
EMIRATES

SAUDI ARABIA

RED SEA

Venetian Glass,
Decorated with
Aventurine
(Goldstone)

Italian Metalized
Plastic 'Gold'

Italian Coral from
Torre del Greco
on the Bay of Naples

Yemeni Silver
with Granulation

YEMEN

ATLANTIC
OCEAN

From Neolithic times, the skills of the beadmaker have flourished and proliferated in Europe and the Middle East. Glass was the most common material, but beads of amber, jet, gold, silver, bronze, and semiprecious stones all show that these cultures had reached the point where the population's resources could be pooled to support the work of full-time craftsmen.

During the thirteenth century, traders and explorers such as Marco Polo brought tales of exotic lands. A century later, the Italian Renaissance had kindled a flowering of the arts and an interest in the classical style of ancient Greece and Rome. By the start of the sixteenth century, Europeans had girdled the globe with trade routes, their sailing ships bringing the resources of the world home to a public eager for novelty. It was during this period that the great centers of glassmaking, stonecutting, and jewelry-making flourished, and some, like Venice, still continue their beadmaking traditions today. Skills were handed down the generations, and while some were jealously guarded, others were traded and refined as technological innovations were adopted.

Today's successors to those early craftsmen are still making beads: Greece has a strong tradition of working in ceramics and metal, while Austria continues a glassmaking industry once

Previous pages Clockwise from top left: Yemeni silver and red amber; Baltic amber; Venetian glass; German semiprecious stones from Idar-Oberstein; rare white coral from the Bay of Naples.

Above right Amber and silver jewellery on sale from a stall in a Yemeni souk.
Above A Turkish pendant with eye beads, talismans against the Evil Eye.
Left Antique 1850s French beaded purse, stitched with tiny glass seed beads.
Right Venetian beads: millefiori, lamp wound, foiled matte, and floral decorated.

centered in Bohemia, France makes glass beads and rocailles, Spain manufactures maiolica pearls, a popular substitute for natural or cultured pearls, Germany's wooden beads are a spin-off from its wooden toymaking tradition, and in Italy new bead designs, using both metals and plastics, are constantly evolving.

The Middle East, at the center of many of the world's great trading routes, was uniquely placed to learn from the beadmaking skills of Africa, India, and the Far East, to embellish and enhance them with Islamic tradition.

Venice and the Island of Murano

Venice was one of the most prosperous and powerful city-states of the Italian Renaissance. Built in a lagoon at the head of the Adriatic Sea, it flourished as a gateway to the riches of the Orient. One of the city's most lucrative industries was glassmaking, and by the mid-fourteenth century Venice had become the undisputed world capital of glass.

Ancient techniques from Phoenicia and Egypt were refined. At first, glass beads were produced to imitate jewels, but the wave of religious fervor that followed the Crusades meant that rosary beads were produced in vast quantities. The ruling doges recognized that they had a unique product to sell, and glassmaking secrets were guarded on pain of death.

The furnaces posed such a fire risk that in 1292 glassworking was confined to the nearby island of Murano. It was there, in the mid-fifteenth century, that Barovier, a master cane-maker, developed glass canes in overlaid colors, the forerunners of the famous chevron or rosetta beads favored by the African trade.

Another of the great names in Venetian glass was Giorgio Ballarin ("the lame one"). As a boy he was a sweeper in Barovier's workshop and was thought to be simple because of his lameness. However, Ballarin watched all the secret glassmaking recipes as they were being made and wrote them down, later opening his own workshop. He became the first major bead producer in Venice, and by the time he died, he was very rich indeed. By then, the city was the finest beadmaking center in the world, a position it continued to hold for centuries.

Above left Venetian beads including wound, feathered, and foiled.
Left The Grand Canal. In 1292 glassmakers moved to Murano to reduce fire risk.

Above Glassworkers wear makeshift clothing such as wool mittens and cardboard arm shields to protect themselves from the searing heat.

Chevron, Rosetta, or Star Beads

With its distinctive V pattern, the chevron is perhaps the aristocrat of beads (*see page 20*). The cane is built up with layers of different-colored glass, classically in red, white, and blue. Molten glass is gathered onto a blowpipe, and a bubble is blown into it to produce a central hole when the cane is drawn out.

The *maestro* smoothes the gather on a slab of iron (a *bronzino*) before dipping it into molten glass of a different color. After rolling it on the *bronzino* again, he plunges the mass into a star-shaped mold, then dips it into molten glass of a second contrasting color. This process is repeated until the desired number of layers is achieved, frequently six. An assistant then places an iron rod with a small amount of molten glass on one end of the cylinder. They walk apart, drawing the molten glass into a cane, which is cooled and cut into shorter lengths. Bead-sized pieces are cut, then the ends are ground on a wheel to form a cylinder, revealing the inner colors.

Millefiori

One of the most famous and decorative of all Venetian beads is the millefiori ("a thousand flowers"). Millefiori canes are produced in all sizes and colors in the same way as those for chevron beads, although they are drawn out to a smaller diameter. Most are made without a central hole because each cane becomes just one component of a finished bead. The tiny slices are fused onto a molten glass base, creating bright floral patterns. The hot bead is pressed in a mold to give it its final shape, cooled, then immersed in acid to free the wire.

Blown Glass Beads

Blown glass beads, like spectacular Christmas decorations, are a fragile example of the bead-maker's art. The glassmaker gathers a small lump of molten glass on the end of a blowpipe and gently inflates it to the required size. Other colors or fine lines of gold are laid across the surface of the bead in spirals by twisting the molten beads as they are blown, producing the characteristic swirls. Finally, each bead is carefully pierced to produce a hole for threading.

Lampwork and Wound Glass Beads

In the Czech Republic and southern Germany, beadmakers, working from home, have made lamp beads for centuries, using molds for correct size and shape. This was also the tradition in Venice and Murano, but nowadays beads are made mainly in workshops. Lamp beads, or *perle à lume*, are always individually hand-made by skilled artisans. The "lamp" is the heat source used to melt the glass cane so it can be wound around a copper rod, producing a wound bead that can then be decorated. The beadworker holds a copper rod in one hand, turning it continuously while heating one end of a glass cane in the other. When the cane is

Left Blown glass beads from Murano, including *filigrana* with its swirled pattern, and other brightly colored designs with gold leaf from various periods.
Right Strings of finest Venetian beads, showing *fiorate* wound glass beads, probably 1830s, with polychrome trailed and dragged decoration, interspersed with transparent and faceted glass beads. Also shown are plain glass beads and contemporary two-tone glass beads.
Below A glassworker at a workshop on Murano, making lampwork wound glass beads.

glowing brilliant orange red, it can be wound around the rod, a deft twist making sure just the correct amount is placed. Later the beads are immersed in acid to dissolve the metal, leaving the hole through the center of the bead.

The beadmakers sit in front of a heat source, a number of fierce gas jets, protected by a glass pane. They wear makeshift protective devices to shield themselves from the heat and, in their wool mittens, cardboard arm shields, bandaging, and sleeves cut out of old sweaters, they look a very raggedy lot. Yet they are superb artists, producing some of the finest examples of Venice's extraordinary output.

Aventurine or Goldstone

Any glass bead with a coppery color glinting on its surface or in its pattern contains aventurine glass. As its name suggests, aventurine (*a ventura*, "by chance") was discovered, apparently by accident, in a Murano workshop during the seventeenth century. Although it bears the same name as a semiprecious stone, it is a man-made composition of glass. Tiny copper crystals are suspended in a glass base, then the raw aventurine is processed into canes, drawn out into flat sections like ribbons, then applied as decorations to the beads. Once, only the most skilled glassmakers knew this closely guarded secret, thus giving Venice a monopoly, although nowadays it is produced elsewhere.

Decorative Bead Finishes

Like most Venetian glasswork, Venetian beads are intended to dazzle the eye, and so are often opulently decorated. Vibrant colors glow up from the depths of a foiled bead, in which the

Above Glass canes used to decorate *fiorate* beads.

glass mantle covers a core of gold or silver foil. Others have gold leaf applied to the surface while molten. Frosted beads are immersed in an acid bath to give a matte finish. A crumbed bead is one that has been rolled in powdered glass while still hot. A plain glass bead may be enhanced with a trail of molten glass in a second color dribbled across its surface: the trail can then be feathered by pulling it down to create a distinctive zigzag pattern. A fusion of color can be created in one bead by melting two canes of glass into a single sphere.

Identifying Venetian Beads

Identifying the origins of a specific bead design can be confusing. Each beadmaking region had its own indigenous style, yet the most popular designs were blatantly copied from other areas, especially Venice. Recipes for glass, however, remained exclusive, and so it is possible, by analyzing the chemical content of the glass, to identify a bead's provenance. But even this can cause some confusion, since many of the European glass and beadmaking centers were set up by immigrant Venetians, who passed on their specialized knowledge.

18

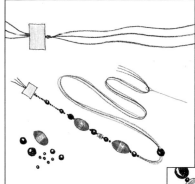

1 Join the 3 strands of thread with a knot and tape to the work surface. Thread on 14 rocailles, 1 round ¼ inch bead, 8 rocailles, and another ¼ inch bead. Then thread, interspersed with rocailles, 1 of each of the following beads: transparent, ⅜ inch, oval Venetian, ⅜ inch, transparent, ¼ inch, oval Venetian, ¼ inch, transparent, ⅜ inch.

2 Separate the 3 strands and thread each with 4 rocailles, 1 ¼ inch bead, and 4 rocailles. Bring the 3 strands together and thread on 1 transparent bead, 1 rocaille, 1 oval bead, 1 rocaille, and 1 transparent bead. Separate the strands and thread each as before. Join the 3 strands and thread on a ⅜ inch bead, a transparent bead, and a ¼ inch round bead, interspersed with rocailles. Separate the strands and thread each with 12 rocailles. Join the strands and thread on an ⅜ inch bead, an oval bead, and the ½ inch bead.

Materials

339 black rocailles, ¹⁄₁₆ inch

13 round black glass beads, ¼ inch

12 faceted transparent glass beads, ¼ inch

12 faceted black glass beads, ⅜ inch

7 oval Venetian glass beads, ¾ inch

15 faceted black glass beads, ¼ inch

1 faceted black glass bead, ½ inch

4 yards fine thread, cut into 3 equal lengths

1 barrel clasp

beading needle

masking tape

clear glue

Total length: 23 inches, plus the 4-inch tassel

3 (Right) To form the tassel, thread onto each of the 3 strands 30 rocailles, 1 round ¼ inch bead, 1 rocaille, 1 faceted ¼ inch bead, 1 rocaille, 1 faceted ⅜ inch bead, and a last rocaille.

Art Deco Venetian Glass Necklace

This necklace, with its spectacular Venetian lampwork beads, is a fine example of Art Deco design. The geometric shapes of the faceted Czech black glass beads and rocailles separate the highly decorated Venetian oval blue beads, which are excellent examples of the typical *fiorate* glass technique, with polychrome trailed decoration.

As with all the projects in this book, we would recommend that you adapt the design according to any number and style of beads that you might be able to find. This elegant necklace is part of a private collection in London.

4 (Left) Pass the thread back up through the tassel strand, the ½ inch bead, the oval Venetian glass bead, and the faceted ⅜ inch bead. Leave the loose end until you have created the remaining 2 tassels in the same way. Gather the 3 loose threads together again and repeat the sequence in reverse to form the other side of the necklace.

5 When the necklace is complete, tie the triple thread to one side of the clasp with an overhand knot. Thread the loose ends back through the last few beads and knot them around the main thread. Dab a spot of glue onto the knot and let it dry before cutting off the ends. Attach the other half of the clasp in the same way.

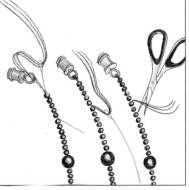

Trade Beads for Africa

Trade beads are usually associated with West Africa where they are most often found, but they were originally created in Venice, Bohemia, and Holland. It is a sorry history—from the end of the fifteenth century, Portuguese trading ships arrived on the coast of West Africa to exploit its treasures: gold, slaves, ivory, and palm oil. Beads were a major component of the currency exchanged for people and products.

Over the next four centuries, millions of beads were traded into Africa, and by the nineteenth century, European beadmakers were

producing a huge variety of designs specifically for the African trade: millefiori, chevrons, striped melons, feather, and eye beads.

In the early 1900s, J. F. Sick & Co., which was first based in Hamburg and later in Amsterdam, worked as bead broker for a Murano company. It had offices in Africa and in Venice, and in 1964, when it closed its Murano office, a vast accumulation of about 21,000 sample beads, housed in a 213-drawer cabinet, was sent to the Royal Tropical Institute in Amsterdam. Another group of similar beads—the Levin Collection—is kept in the British Museum, London. Both collections form a priceless record of an important artistic heritage. Hidden in dusty corners of old Venetian and Muranese workshops, it is still possible to find examples of the beads that crossed the world and made white traders rich. Once considered to have no great intrinsic value, these beads are now highly desirable.

Far left Bella woman, Upper Volta, in old Czech molded glass beads. *Left, from top* Venetian trade beads: sixteenth-century 7-layer chevrons; wound glass beads with polychrome decoration (also seen below); and curved millefiori chips. *Above* Trade beads in a market in Accra, Ghana.

Trade beads are now eagerly collected by bead lovers from all over the world. Local bead traders purchase them from the very villages that used to be at the center of the slave trade. They are rethreaded onto raffia strings and sold to importers in the United States and Europe, with some of the rarest varieties commanding considerable sums.

Above A necklace of trade beads that have been sliced into smaller pieces, then strung together with large red glass oval beads from Holland.

Right These two strands of Venetian glass trade beads, probably 1850s, show different styles of wound beads (bicones and cylinders) with fine polychrome decoration. The bicones are now being copied by West African beadmakers using recycled glass.

Coral Beads from the Bay of Naples

On the southern shores of the Bay of Naples lie the ruins of Pompeii and Herculaneum, the two ancient Roman cities buried in A.D. 79 by debris from the erupting Mt. Vesuvius. Nearby is the town of Torre del Greco, the center of the Mediterranean coral industry where, for centuries, the coral fishing boats have landed their strange harvest.

At the time of the Inquisition, Naples was under the influence of Spain. The coral craftsmen were mostly Jewish, carving coral for the Church, the major patron for such exquisite works of art. However, together with their co-religionists in the Spanish dominions, the Jews of Naples were expelled, but over the years they slowly drifted back to continue their work under later rulers.

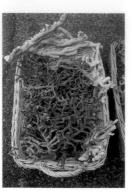

Left Raw branch coral from Torre del Greco on the Bay of Naples.
Right These necklaces from around the world show the versatility of coral.
Below The process of cutting and carving branch coral into beads.

By the eighteenth century, thousands of workshops in Torre del Greco were turning out beads, carvings, jewelry, and cameos.

In the past, coral was fished from boats dragging a heavy iron cross called a *salabra* from which dangled a mesh of cords. The coral branches growing on the rocks were snapped off and became entangled in the mesh. Nowadays, coral is fished rather too efficiently, either by ships using a more sophisticated apparatus (the *ingegno*) or by divers who literally clean the coral off the rocks as much as 250–400 feet below the surface. Considering that a branch of coral (such as the one shown left) can take up to 250 years to grow to that size, it is not surprising that a shortage is imminent.

Coral is found all along the North African coast, from Morocco to Tunisia, but much of the coral sold today comes from the Pacific, especially around Japan. Pacific coral is much larger than the Mediterranean variety, so it can

be carved into larger items. It is distinguished by the white matrix, known by the Italians as *fiore bianca, or* "white flower", inside the stalk. Today, even in Torre del Greco, most of the coral is of oriental origin, and many local coral craftsmen have turned to other work.

Coral Beadmaking

In spite of the decline of the coral industry in Italy, some beads are still made there. However, it is a skilled job, and the tiniest beads are now almost unobtainable because of the delicate workmanship required. Workers always specialize in one operation, although they should know and understand how to carry out all the other stages of production.

The raw coral is first soaked in hydrochloric acid for several minutes to remove its calcific skin. The cutter then studies the branch to work out the optimum way of achieving as many cuttings as possible.

The branch is cut into blanks. Each blank is held in a vise, drilled, quickly held against a grinder for shaping, then polished by tumbling in a drum with water and pumice.

The beads are strung and graded according to color, and sizes are measured to a quarter of a millimeter, a task requiring great skill.

Below Coral, always highly valued, has also been widely copied in glass. These attractive examples were made in Holland and Czechoslovakia.

Amber: Gold of the North

Baltic amber is the fossilized resin from pine trees that grew in northern Europe some 40 million years ago. It ranges in color from a pale candied honey to the deep golden red of Indian tea. It sometimes includes the fossilized remains of plants and insects.

Amber has been used to make jewelry since Neolithic times, and has been found in ancient graves all over Europe, dating back to 15,000 B.C. Etruscans, Phoenicians, Greeks, and Romans all promoted the popularity of amber, and a great ancient trading route, the Via Ambra, wound its way from the shores of the Baltic to the Mediterranean at Trieste.

Farther afield, the peoples of China, the Himalaya, Persia, Turkey, and the Arab world held amber in high esteem, incorporating it into their traditional jewelry. It is of great importance in Somalia, Morocco, and Egypt, where amber beads can be massive, eye-catching, and spectacular.

The stories of gathering, trading, and bartering of Baltic amber can make vivid reading. For example, in medieval times, amber floating in the sea was gathered in nets attached to poles, hooked out from under submerged boulders – or even retrieved by divers. Stormy weather often dislodged chunks from the seabed, which would then be washed up on shore. Even now, after a storm, the beaches of England and Denmark occasionally yield a treasured lump.

Baltic amber is mined in Lithuania, Poland, and the Russian Federation, and other sources include Sicily, Burma (a deep red variety), Mexico, and Japan. Recently amber was discovered in the Dominican Republic, containing more fossilized remains of small animals, plants, and insects than is found in Baltic amber.

Authenticating Amber

There is a foolproof way to test if a piece of amber is genuine. Put water in a bowl, dissolve salt until it will dissolve no more. Add the amber: if it sinks, it is plastic, if it floats, it is true amber. That is why amber floats in the sea.

Another test is to rub your finger vigorously against the amber until it becomes uncomfortably hot. Quickly sniff the amber: you should be able to detect a piney, resinous, aromatic smell.

Above Copenhagen in Denmark, with an excellent Amber Museum and numerous amber shops.

Right Baltic amber chips. Similar strings have been discovered in many prehistoric sites in Scandinavia.

Far left A pendant of three beads in different ambers. *This page* Baltic amber containing occlusions where air has become compressed creating leaflike structures.

Victorian Jet

In 1861 Queen Victoria's husband, Prince Albert, died, and the Queen entered a protracted period of mourning. Her subjects around the world followed suit, and if they, unlike the Queen, gave up wearing black after the appropriate period, many of them continued to honor the Prince Consort by wearing black jewelry. That jewelry was made of jet from Whitby in North Yorkshire, England, and it was so admired that the French later developed a glass known as "French jet."

Jet is an extraordinary and ancient substance. Amber was formed perhaps 40 million years ago, but jet began forming and fossilizing during the Jurassic Period, 208–144 million years ago. In the same type of jungles that formed amber, another species of ancient tree was flourishing, similar to today's *Araucaria* or monkey puzzle tree. When the trees died and fell, slowly, like coal, the tree fossilized into a kind of brown coal called lignite. Prehistoric man used the hard substance to carve ornaments and beads.

Although it was well known and worked during the Bronze Age, Roman, and medieval times, it was from 1840 to 1920 that the fashion for jet was at its height, and Whitby became the

Top left The jet-producing lias seams in the cliff faces near Whitby in Yorkshire.
Left, from center Jet in various stages of production from raw material to faceted beads.

Right This fine antique dress ornament is in the butterfly design typical of Art Nouveau. The butterfly was pinned to the bodice and the long, fine tassels swung free to thigh level.

center of a thriving industry. The two shops in the town in 1832 grew to over 200 by 1872, employing more than 1,500 men, women, and children. With some justification, local people claim that their jet is the finest in the world (other famous sites are in Spain, Saxony, the Aude and Languedoc in France, with further deposits in Russia, China, and California).

In Yorkshire the lias, or seam, about 13,000 feet thick, is divided into three layers, the Upper, Middle, and Lower, and it is from the Upper one that the best-quality jet was mined. It was midnight black, with a brilliant luster and velvety sheen when polished, smooth to the touch, entirely opaque, and light in weight.

Jet mining was a hazardous job, and many accidents occurred in the semi-darkness of the pits as men crawled with crude lamps giving out little light. Jet was transported by pack-horse to the dealers in Whitby, who sold it on to the hundreds of jet workers. It is amazing, considering the fragile nature of the material, how intricately it could be carved and the delicacy of the designs inscribed into its smooth surface. Workers treasured their tools—they were usually homemade and were often handed down from father to son.

Beads were difficult to make since they were awkward to grip, and many a jet worker had sore and bleeding fingers. Sometimes, in order to protect their fingers, they put melted ocka-matutt, which is a mixture of shellac and glue, as hot as they could bear, on the tips of their fingers, covering them with a thin cotton bandage. They used a fine point, sometimes made from an umbrella spoke, to drill the holes. Often strings of jet beads could be as long as 5 feet, each bead

faceted with up to a hundred facings. For almost a century, there was a thriving industry in Whitby. But suddenly, as so often happens, fashion changed; by 1920 demand had almost died away, and all the skilled workers, miners, and shopkeepers had to seek other work.

The mines all lie deserted now, and the skill and expertise of jet carving died away with the last trained craftsman in 1958, though a few carvers still practise the art in the town using jet picked up on the shore.

Above Mid-nineteenth century jet necklaces made from true Whitby jet. Black mourning jewelry became highly fashionable after the death of Prince Albert in 1861. The French copied these designs in glass, and such faux jet should be labeled "French jet" or "French glass."

Faux Jet

While the fashion for jet was at its height, many other materials were carved and fashioned in such a way as to give the appearance of jet. Though beads made in this way were not necessarily intended to deceive, nowadays they may be unwittingly mislabeled as jet. When true jet is rubbed with fine sandpaper, it produces a brown dust. It also has a conchoidal (shell-like) fracture and chips like glass, producing a clean edge that can be seen with a magnifying glass.

French jet could be mass-produced and it became extremely popular, especially since the tiny beads used for trimming dresses could be more easily manufactured.

A more difficult material to distinguish from true jet, however, is vulcanite, rubber that has been hardened by being heated with sulfur. As vulcanite will also produce brown dust when rubbed with sandpaper, the only true test is to apply a hot needle to the surface of the bead. If it is made from vulcanite, it will smell of rubber.

Bakelite, one of the first plastics, can only be distinguished from jet by the black, rather than brown, dust given off when rubbed.

Easier to spot is bog oak, a fossilized dark brown wood that was often carved into the mourning designs popular in Ireland in the 1850s. Its dark brown color and wood grain betray its true identity. Other imitators were English cannel coal and *gutta percha*, the resin of a type of Malaysian rubber tree. Nowadays, cameos based on original jet designs are generally made from epoxy resin, but these are not intended to deceive since they are made in molds and lack the sheen of true jet.

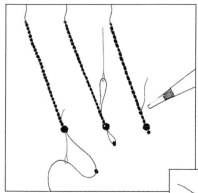

1 To make the tassel, cut 7 strands of thread 14 inches long. Make a knot 2½ inches from the end of 1 strand and attach the needle to the other end. Thread on 49 hexagonal beads, a ⅛ inch faceted round bead, and a further hexagonal bead. Pass your thread around the last bead and back up through 2 or 3 hexagonal

beads, then tie a knot over the main thread and secure it with glue; cut off the ends. Make the other 6 strands in the same way.

2 Cut a thread 2½ yards long and thread up 38 small round beads, interspersed with hexagonal beads. Then thread the following: 1 bicone, 1 small round bead, 2 hexagonal beads, 1 small round bead, 1 large round bead, 1 small round bead, 2 hexagonal beads, 1 small round bead, 1 bicone, 1 small round bead, 3 hexagonal beads, 5 small round beads interspersed with hexagonal beads, 3 hexagonal beads, 1 small round bead, 1 large round bead, and 1 small round bead.

3 Gather the 7 strands of the tassel and tie them together with 2 overhand knots as close to the last beads as possible. Secure the knot with glue and let it dry before cutting off the ends. Attach to the main necklace by passing the needle through the knot and back up through the last 3 beads.

Jet Necklace

Jet necklaces were at the height of British fashion during the Victorian era. They could be up to a yard in length, worn doubled over or knotted. This simple, elegant necklace with its tassel decoration is typical of the style of the time. It has been made from an assortment of carved jet beads, some of which are so small it is difficult to believe they were made by hand. It is still possible to find these beads in antique markets, very often in a sorry heap of broken threads, and this is the ideal opportunity to buy a selection to make into a necklace. This necklace was constructed from beads found in a market by an aficionado of old beads.

Hint
This necklace could be constructed in a number of ways, but you will probably find it easiest to make the tassel first, then attach it to the center of the necklace as you thread it up. This way you can make sure that the tassel hangs properly.

4 Gently pull the thread taut, easing the top of the tassel flush up to the base of the last small round bead. Thread up the other half of the necklace, reversing the pattern of the beads and ending with a hexagonal bead. Tie the ends together with two firm knots, apply a dab of glue, and leave it to dry before cutting off the ends.

Materials

453 hexagonal jet beads,
    ⅟₁₆ inch
105 faceted round jet
    beads, about ⅛ inch
4 faceted jet bicones,
    ¾ inch
3 faceted round jet beads,
    ⅜ inch

5½ yards fine strong thread,
    such as button thread
beading needle
clear glue
*Total length: 30 inches, plus
    the 4-inch tassel*

The Glassmakers of Bohemia

The former Central European kingdom of Bohemia is now part of the new Czech Republic. It has changed rulers many times over the centuries—annexed into the Holy Roman Empire in 1355 and controlled by the Hapsburgs from 1526. However, in spite of continually changing foreign influences, its unique cultural identity continued to flourish. Recent excavations show that glassmaking began there as long ago as the beginning of the fourteenth century. The Bohemian Forest and Bavarian area, with its plentiful supply of minerals as well as wood to fire the furnaces, was the ideal situation for a glassworking and beadmaking industry.

Much of the work was done by villagers and peasants at home. Using simple molds and gas-fired lamps, they were the backbone of Czech bead production. In 1945 the new Communist government nationalized the whole industry, forming a massive state organization, Jablonex,

Opposite Molded and faceted Bohemian glass beads from the 1930s.
Left Jablonek, the "glass capital" of the Czech Republic, site of Jablonex, the nationalized company created by the communist government in 1945. Since the fall of communism in Eastern Europe, the industry has been privatized.
Above Fifteenth-century Czech molded trade beads, once thought to have been made in Africa.
Right The Czech Republic produces fine faceted and foiled glass beads in a huge range of colors. Their output rivals in volume the production of Japan, and of Swarovski in Austria.

exporting around the world. Now, however, private enterprise is flourishing once more.

Czech glass beads, like Venetian, are world-renowned. Quality of design, workmanship, and marketing has meant there has always been a great demand for these products.

Czech beads have a universal appeal, and favored styles vary from imitations of natural stones to beads as brightly colored beads as hard candy. Always innovative with their designs, Czechs are particularly adept at cutting beads and grinding facets. It is their talent with special coatings and finishes, foil centers, as well as the manufacture of flower beads that keeps them in constant competition with Venice. However, in spite of a seemingly endless stream of new designs, beads in many of the old patterns are still produced, and the reputation of Czech beads is still as high as it ever was.

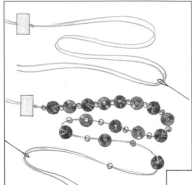

1 Double each length of thread. Thread 1 with the needle, tie a loose knot 6 inches from the other end and tape it to the work surface. Starting and finishing with a transparent rocaille, thread on 36 colored beads, alternating with rocailles; tape or loosely knot the end. Make the other 4 strands with 39, 42, 45, and 48 colored beads.

2 Lay the completed strands out on the work surface and make sure they lie well together. To attach the necklace to the clasp, thread the needle to the longest strand and thread on a length of gimp so that it lies just above the last rocaille. Pass the needle through the top loop of the box clasp and then back through the last 3 beads.

3 Pull gently and the gimp will ease into a loop around the clasp's metal loop. Unthread the needle, separate the 2 strands and knot them twice around the main thread. Do not cut off the loose ends until all 5 strands are attached. Repeat the process to secure the other end of the strand to the corresponding loop on the other half of the clasp.

Czech Glass Five-Stranded Necklace

The 1950s heralded a new wave of colorful glass bead designs, inspired by the innovative jewelry creations of French couturier Christian Dior. Decorative and opulent, his designs marked a move towards geometric shapes and clean-cut lines, increasing the popularity of cut glass. This necklace is a sophisticated example of a simple shape that has been made up in a number of glittering colors. The five strands hang close to the neckline and the cut-glass beads are interspersed with small plain glass rocailles, which help to set off their shape.

Hints

This necklace uses a gimp to protect the threads from chafing on the metal loops of the clasp and to provide a neat finish. The original (right) uses an 11-strand box clasp with the strands 1 or 2 holes apart.

4 Attach the other 4 strands to the clasp the same way, making sure you attach the graduated lengths to the correct loops, with the shortest attached to the bottom loop. Test the lie of the necklace and make any adjustments. Secure all the knots with a dab of glue and let it dry before snipping off the loose ends.

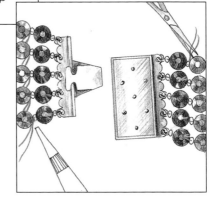

Materials

210 cut-glass beads, in
    amethyst, emerald, topaz,
    and vitrail light, ¼ x ⅜ inch
215 transparent rocailles,
    ⅛ inch
8¾ yards thread, cut into 5
    lengths of 1¾ yards each
3 inches gimp, cut into 10
    lengths of ⅜ inch each
5-strand box clasp,
    ⅝ x 1 inch

beading needle
masking tape
clear glue
Total length:
    15 inches (shortest strand),
    20 inches (longest strand)

Stonecutting in the Rhineland

Idar-Oberstein in the German Rhineland has been a stonecutting center since the fifteenth century. Local deposits of agate and quartz were mined by early beadmakers, the power for their grinding wheels coming from the River Nahe. Nowadays, though eclipsed by the vast output of the Chinese and Indian factories, it is still an important stone center.

The early beadmakers gradually perfected their skills and techniques, learning about cutting, coloring, and drilling, creating new shapes and patterns for beads, and all the while improving the traditional methods used to enhance the natural colors and markings.

Soon the area became a major force in the African trade in stone beads, which had previously been dominated by the 5,000-year-old stonecutting industry of Cambay in India. From 1830 to the 1970s, 100 million beads were produced in Germany for export to Africa.

Above A necklace of cornelian disks and tubes made in Idar-Oberstein. The stones were probably made for export to Africa. Cornelian was formerly mined near the town, though the deposits have now been exhausted.

Left This painting in the museum at Idar-Oberstein shows the stonecutters lying prone on their benches, faces just inches from the grinding wheels.

The stonecutters worked lying prone on benches in front of huge, water-driven grinding wheels. The wheels had grooves cut into them, which meant the worker could make beads of various sizes, while a steady drip of water kept the stones cool as they were worked. In this uncomfortable manner, they produced a selection of shapes that were later converted into beads and carvings.

Local deposits of stone are now exhausted, and supplies are imported from southern Brazil and Northern Uruguay. Today, Idar-Oberstein is still one of the most important centers in the history of beads, and the museum has excellent displays of great interest to the bead aficionado.

Above Purple amethyst crystals are found inside smooth, pale, hollow rocks, or "vughs". Their colors range from pale mauve to darkest purple.

Above and below Amethyst "chip" beads (top) made from scraps resulting from the production of the fine round beads such as those shown below

Right Well-crafted banded agate beads in graduating sizes, each one cut so the "white" bands are seen around the "equator" (center) of each bead.

Amethyst: Queen of Semiprecious Stones

Amethyst is a Greek word meaning "not drunk," and the stone was formerly used as a talisman against drunkenness.

The stone is violet or purple in color, comprized of quartz formed from silica, and found inside the hollow interiors of smooth geode rock, known as "vughs." When opened, these outwardly dull rocks are lined with a mass of crystals in many shades of violet.

Although the Idar-Oberstein area has now been outstripped by Brazil as a major source of amethyst, many other countries also mine the purple crystal. Russia, North America, South Africa, India, Japan, and Australia all have deposits of varying importance. It was even found on the tiny English Channel Island of Sark, though the supplies there have also been exhausted and tourists who buy souvenir "Sark stones" are in fact buying Brazilian amethyst.

Chalcedony, Agates, and Other Quartzes

Chalcedony is the family name of a whole range of quartzes. The group includes agate (banded from cream to brown) and its varieties such as cornelian (red), moss agate (greenish), chrysoprase (black or green), sard (brownish yellow), onyx (varying from black and white to gray and white), and plasma (green). A few lesser-known quartzes are also included in this family group.

Although these quartzes are all essentially composed of the same elements, the geological conditions under which they formed varied in terms of temperature and pressure, as well as the injection of trace minerals, giving the stunning variety of colors we see today.

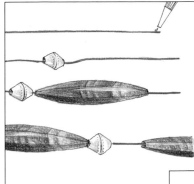

1 Lay out the cornelian bicones, placing the largest in the center and graduating to the smallest at both ends. Stiffen about 2½ inches of one end of the thread with glue. Tape the other end to the work surface, then thread on a silver bicone followed by the smallest cornelian tube. String the cornelian bicones, alternating them with silver bicones.

Faceted Cornelian from Idar-Oberstein

This necklace, made of skillfully cut cornelian bicones, bears all the hallmarks of the craftspeople of Idar-Oberstein. The perfection of these facets makes the beads shine so that they almost appear to have been moulded, yet each bead has been gently abraded against the grinding wheel many times in hours of painstaking work in order to create its many facets.

Although they were primarily made for the African market, this type of bead is now highly collectable in the West and is one of the designs eagerly imported back from Africa.

2 When you have threaded on the final silver bead, hold up the necklace. When you are satisfied that the cornelian bicones are lying symmetrically, join both sides of the necklace with 2 overhand knots close to the last beads. The string should not be rigidly taut, but it should not be so loosely knotted that gaps can be seen between the beads.

3 Apply a dab of glue to the knots to secure them and let it dry. To finish off neatly, pass both threads, one at a time, down through a silver bead and a cornelian bicone.

Hints

Handle the beads with care since they chip easily, and use strong thread so that the sharp holes do not fray it. As the beads are long, it may be easier to stiffen one end of the thread by dragging it through a drop of glue on some scrap paper, instead of using a needle.

4 Tie the strands around the main thread with a neat double knot. Carefully apply a drop of clear glue to secure the knot and let it dry before cutting off the loose ends.

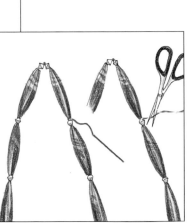

Materials

17 cornelian bicones,
   1¾–2½ inches

18 silver bicones, ⅜ inch

1½ yards strong linen
   thread

clear glue

masking tape

Total length: 39 inches

The Middle East

The ancient trading routes, from Yemen to Saudi Arabia, throughout the Persian Gulf into Turkey, Israel, and Lebanon, guaranteed a two-way flow of goods and ideas between India and the Far East and Egypt, Africa, and the Mediterranean. Bead pattern and design followed the same route.

Silverwork from Yemen has overtones of Indian traditions, although refined and stylized by different influences, particularly Islam. The nomadic Bedouin tribes treated their jewelry as portable wealth, carrying with them finely decorated silver beads and their traditional necklaces, often bearing the *hirz*, a cylindrical pendant containing verses from the Koran. This practice had come from Persia (now Iran) in the second and third centuries.

The important glassmaking tradition based at Hebron in Israel was disseminated over the centuries as far as Cairo and Turkey, only to return to its birthplace fifty years ago when families returned to their roots in the newly formed state of Israel. The heavy glass Hebron beads are now much prized by collectors.

Charms and amulets have a deep significance in many parts of this region. Eye beads have a particular role to play in warding off the malevolent magic of the Evil Eye. Beautiful blue eye beads are produced from glass made using mineral salts from the Dead Sea, while in the countries which border Afghanistan, blue faience beads – an early form of glazed clay – are used extensively to protect animals, especially donkeys, the major form of transportation.

The souk, the traditional marketplace of the Arab world, is an irresistible hunting ground for bead enthusiasts. Here the smells, sounds, and sights that assail the senses become almost secondary to the excitement of discovery. In the winding mazes of covered alleyways filled with veiled shoppers, stalls display assorted necklaces of silver beads, coins, amber and coral, filigree beads from Kuwait, Oman, and Saudi Arabia, or beautiful bridal necklaces, known as *Iqd*, from Yemen.

Above This necklace of Iranian blue frit beads is interspersed with blue glass bicones.

Above The Imam's palace at Wadi Dhar in Yemen.
Below left A shop in the souk at Thula, near Sana'a in Yemen. Middle Eastern souks are exciting and rewarding hunting grounds for the bead buyers
Right From left, Turkish eye beads, Hebron glass beads, and blue faience.
Far Right Made by Jewish craftsmen, Yemeni necklaces often include an amulet holder, which would contain either a verse from the Koran or a Jewish marriage certificate.

Africa

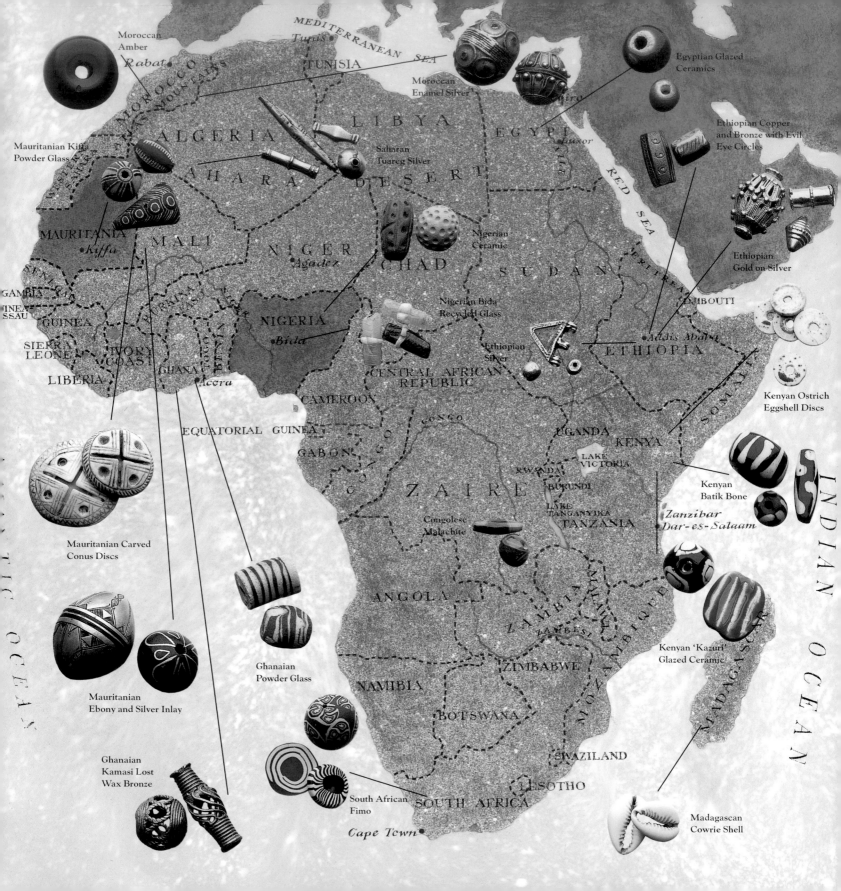

Moroccan
Amber

MEDITERRANEAN SEA

Tunis

TUNISIA

Moroccan
Enamel Silver

Egyptian Glazed
Ceramics

Mauritanian Kiffa
Powder Glass

MOROCCO

Rabat

ATLAS MOUNTAINS

ALGERIA

LIBYA

SAHARA

Luxor

EGYPT

Cairo

NILE

RED SEA

ERITREA

Ethiopian Copper
and Bronze with Evil
Eye Circles

Saharan
Tuareg Silver

DESERT

Ethiopian
Gold on Silver

WESTERN SAHARA

MAURITANIA

kiffa

MALI

NIGER

Agadez

CHAD

SUDAN

Nigerian Ceramic

DJIBOUTI

Addis Ababa

ETHIOPIA

SOMALIA

Kenyan Ostrich
Eggshell Discs

Nigerian Bida
Recycled Glass

Ethiopian
Silver

SENEGAL

GAMBIA

GUINEA
BISSAU

GUINEA

SIERRA
LEONE

LIBERIA

IVORY
COAST

BURKINA FASO

GHANA

TOGO

BENIN

Accra

NIGERIA

Bida

CAMEROON

EQUATORIAL GUINEA

GABON

CONGO

CENTRAL AFRICAN
REPUBLIC

ZAIRE

UGANDA

LAKE
VICTORIA

RWANDA

BURUNDI

LAKE
TANGANYIKA

KENYA

Kenyan
Batik Bone

Zanzibar
Dar-es-Salaam

INDIAN OCEAN

Mauritanian Carved
Conus Discs

TANZANIA

Congolese
Malachite

Kenyan 'Kazuri'
Glazed Ceramic

Mauritanian
Ebony and Silver Inlay

Ghanaian
Powder Glass

ANGOLA

ZAMBIA

MALAWI

ZAMBESI

MOZAMBIQUE

MADAGASCAR

ATLANTIC OCEAN

ZIMBABWE

NAMIBIA

BOTSWANA

SWAZILAND

Ghanaian
Kamasi Lost
Wax Bronze

South African
Fimo

SOUTH AFRICA

LESOTHO

Madagascan
Cowrie Shell

Cape Town

I t is said that the entire continent of Africa is covered in beads and that you can find them anywhere, abandoned and forgotten, buried in a cemetery, in a riverbed, or on the seashore. That is part myth, part truth. It is true that over the centuries Africa has been the destination of millions and millions of beads, carried there as ballast in ships, as gifts or as currency. Beads were eagerly sought by the Africans for decoration and as a sign of their wealth and status. Different cultures favored different styles; and some traded them, some revered them, and some made their own.

Another myth is that today they can be found anywhere—and for a song. Indigenous African beads have become very fashionable, as have imported European beads. Collectors of old beads have swarmed over the continent, dealers comb the villages, and, although they are still obtainable, beads are not as easy to find as they were twenty years ago and they are far more expensive than they once were. Yet the allure remains: the sheer hubbub of daily life is intoxicating, and the diversity of the peoples is reflected in the complexity and rich variety of their bead-making traditions.

Many very different cultures have evolved across the continent, and links have been forged between many nomadic peoples at ceremonies and fairs.

Previous pages From left: aluminum beads from Kenya's Gabra people, made from cooking pots; silver and amber from Morocco; Ethiopian necklace with coral, silver, and traded Indian coins; Kenyan batik bone; beads of petrified dinosaur droppings.
Above Nigerian Yoruba face motif bag, made with European glass beads.
Left This Tanzanian woman is wearing finely beaded, typically Central African earlobe pendants, necklaces, and bracelets.
Right A Songhai woman from Mali's Bandiagara Plateau, with beads of copper, brass, silver, agate, cornelian, and colored glass.

As a result, their traditional jewelry and adornments absorbed numerous decorative influences from their near neighbors.

Lifestyle and dress have also been affected by two of Africa's main faiths, Christianity and Islam, and religious beliefs are particularly reflected in jewelry design. Many visitors to Africa regret that old traditions, especially in dress, maintained and developed for centuries, are being abandoned. Warriors from isolated tribes, who not long ago sported ash-covered bodies and beads, now wear the T-shirts and scarves brought in by Western traders. With luck, however, Africa's rich heritage will continue to be regarded with pride and its wealth of cultural traditions will be upheld.

Enamel Work from Morocco

Many of the nomadic peoples of North Africa are Berbers, a group with an ancient tradition of silverwork. Over the centuries each tribe has developed its own particular skills and traditions in jewelry making: the Kabyle of Algeria wear brightly enameled silver, in the Middle Atlas the Ait Hadiddu make heavy silver pieces and necklaces with huge amber beads, and on the fringes of the Sahara, exquisite jewellery is created using silver coins, coral branches, amazonite and glass beads, and the "hand of Fatima" pendant, the five fingers of which represent the five fundamental principles of Islam. The styles of individual tribes have gradually become less defined as nomads settle down in villages to ply their trade.

The old walled town of Taroudant, with its groves of orange, lemon, and olive trees, lies near the southwestern edge of the Atlas Mountains. The town has a small, fascinating

Right This Berber woman from Morocco's Atlas Mountains wears a necklace of imitation amber beads interspersed with large silver beads. Her headdress and earrings are made of silver coins.

Above A Haratine woman of the Tissent tribe, wearing jewelry made of silver, coral, and other semi-precious stones, a sign of her husband's wealth.
Left A Berber shepherd tends his flock in the Atlas Mountains of Morocco.
Right Typical Moroccan beads and five-pointed cross, in hand-crafted silver and enamel, filigree, and Tuareg silver cubes.

souk selling food, spices, cosmetics, potions, baskets, and carpets. There are also jewelry and artefact shops full of traditional Berber and Tuareg rings, necklaces, bracelets, earrings, fibulæ, and brooches gathered from the Atlas Mountains and the Sahara Desert.

Taroudant holds a strategic position on the old trading routes to Mauritania, Senegal, and Mali, and many of the formerly nomadic families have settled in surrounding villages where they practice traditional crafts, including bead and jewelry making.

The village of Ouled Tarna is the home of Hamid Abdelaziz, one of the finest craftsmen

in the area. He is a Tuareg who specializes in making beads, including the traditional Berber enameled beads (*kerkoba*), which feature very strongly in Moroccan jewelry. Wearing his long white djellaba and turban, Hamid works in the doorway of his one-story house, taking advantage of the natural light, yet shaded from the sun—the temperature can rise to a stifling 110°F. The butane torch and cylinder are his only concessions to modernity, and all his raw materials, such as the small sheets of silver or other metals, are bought locally.

Using a template and hammer, he cuts out circular pieces of metal to the size required for the bead. The metal pieces are hammered into a concave mold to form hollow half-spheres, then a small hole is punched through the center of each. Next, Hamid painstakingly places small rings and granulations onto each half-sphere in a symmetrical pattern. Each piece is brushed with solder made from silver, copper,

Above and below These Moroccan enameled beads are made in stages. First, circles are stamped out of a thin sheet of metal. The metal is then hammered into a spherical shape. Tiny rings of silver are added for decoration.

Below right Finally, enamel paint is carefully applied to each bead, resulting in a delicate and colorful effect. The enamel is then fired. This process is repeated several times in order to raise the level of enamel. The method is similar to Chinese cloisonné work (see page 108).

and water, and heated over a wide flame to weld the pattern to the bead. Too much or too little heat would ruin the fine work, but he works with great speed and precision. The two halves of the bead are sanded, then soldered together. The bead is then dipped into *sid*, an antiquing solution that oxidizes the metal so that, once polished, the raised designs shine against a dark background.

The final stage is enameling. Glass rocailles are pounded into a fine powder and the pattern filled in by precisely placing the colored powders into the rings. They are then melted into place with a blowtorch.

The same methods can be used to create a wide variety of traditional beads, ranging from the highly decorated, larger *kerkoba* beads used as the eyecatching centerpiece for a necklace to tiny, simple silver beads.

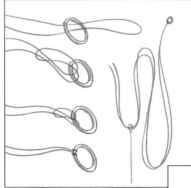

1 Double the thread and pass the folded end through one of the jumprings. Feed the loose ends around the ring and through the end loop, pulling them tight to secure the jumpring to the thread. Tie 2 overhand knots in the doubled thread ⅜ inch from the jumpring, then thread the needle onto the cut ends.

2 Thread on 1 silver polygon, 11 wooden disks, 1 silver round, 11 wooden disks and 1 silver disk. Then, interspersing each with a wooden disk, thread on 1 enamel bead, 1 amber oval, 1 enamel, 1 silver disk, 1 enamel, 1 amber, 1 enamel, 1 silver disk, 1 enamel, 1 amber, 1 enamel. Then add another silver disk and the cross. Reverse the bead sequence to thread up the other side of the necklace.

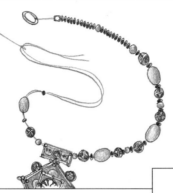

3 Thread on the other jumpring and, leaving a gap of ¼ inch between it and the last bead, pass the needle back through the silver polygon and 3 wooden disks. For the moment, leave the loose ends free.

Moroccan Berber Necklace

This colorful, enameled necklace bears the cross of the Berbers, known as *walataidye*. It is believed to provide protection against the Evil Eye. Such pendants, often incorporating blue glass, which represents the Good Eye and deflects the glance of the Evil Eye, are popular adornments for brides and pregnant women, who are considered most at risk. This example was bought in the Moroccan town of Taroudant, but Berber crosses and enameled beads can also be purchased from antique markets and dealers in African artifacts.

Hint
The heavy beads and cross will need a thick linen (or similar) thread. Use at least double-thickness thread and remember to allow for an extra working length of 12 inches.

4 Starting just above the bead, tightly wind the wire in a spiral around the thread. When you reach the jumpring, cut off the wire and push the end inside the spiral. Knot the loose ends around the main strand, secure with glue, and let it dry before cutting the ends. Repeat on the other side. Use pliers to attach the S-clasp to a jumpring.

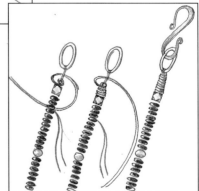

Materials

1 antique Berber cross,
  2½ x 3¼ inches
12 round enamelled beads,
  ½ inch
6 oval amber beads, ¾ inch
8 silver disks, ⅜ inch
66 dark wood disks, ¼ inch
2 round silver beads, ¼ inch
2 polygonal silver beads,
  ¼ inch

2 yards thick linen thread
12 inches fine silver-plated
  wire
2 silver jumprings
1 silver S-clasp
beading needle
needle-nose pliers
clear glue
Total length excluding cross:
  24½ inches

Mauritania

Mauritania is a land of stark contrasts, bordered on the west by the Atlantic Ocean and by the Sahara on the east. Excavations have revealed ancient beads of cowrie and eggshells, jasper, agate and garnet, glass beads from Europe, coral, seeds, gold filigree, and scented beads of sweet-smelling pastes.

Beads made in Mauritania include dark wooden beads inlaid with a pattern of fine silver wire (this page) and Kiffa beads of powdered colored glass (page 42). During the late nineteenth century, the women of Kiffa began making beads in imitation of European millefiori and the ancient Islamic beads *morfia* and *dhar vekrun*. Often working in the desert with nothing more than twigs, needles, and gum arabic, they created beautiful designs now eagerly sought by collectors. Having molded the core from powdered glass, the women used a needle and saliva to decorate it with different colors of powdered glass applied in geometric shapes, such as a blue circle to represent the sky, chevrons for water, and a green circle for hope. Finished beads were arranged on sheets of hot metal, covered with sand and a pottery lid, then fired over a brazier. Beads are now being produced for export, so the skills of the Kiffa women will be preserved.

Below Silver-inlaid wood.

1 Practice turning loops with round-nosed pliers before starting. Using manageable lengths of wire, make a right angle about ¼ inch from one end. Grasping the tip of the wire, turn it up into a neat circle. Thread on a ½ inch bicone and trim the wire, leaving enough to turn a loop on the other side of the bead.

Mauritanian Silver-Inlaid Necklace

Beads of ebony or another dark hardwood, inlaid with a pattern of silver, are typical of Mauritania. Using a small blowtorch to make the wire malleable, the delicate silver swirls are formed with fine pliers and held in place while being tapped carefully into the surface of the wood. The bead is then filed and polished until smooth. This necklace is formed by pinning the beads onto pieces of wire and linking the loops together. The clasp has also been fashioned from wire, illustrating the ingenuity of the artisan in using readily available materials.

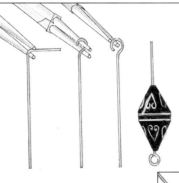

2 (Right) Leave the second loop slightly open until you have hooked it to the loop of the next bead. Turn a loop in the end of another piece of wire and hook it onto the partially opened loop on the first section, then close the loop with pliers. Thread on another bead, cut the wire about ¼ inch above and form another partially opened loop.

3 (Left) Continue this process until 11 of the ½ inch bicones are linked, then add a ⅝ inch bicone, the 1⅛ inch bicone and another of ⅝ inch. Build up the other side of the necklace with the remaining ½ inch beads. If you prefer, complete small sections first and join them together afterward, using equal numbers of each bead on both sides.

Materials

22 inlaid bicones, ½ inch

2 inlaid bicones, ⅝ inch

1 inlaid bicone, 1⅛ inch

1½ yards of fine wire

round-nosed pliers

wire cutters

Total length: 21 inches

4 Once the linking is complete, make the clasp. Cut a length of wire about 2½ inches, fold it in 3, and thread the unfolded end through the last loop on one side. Wind this length around the hook to secure it with whipping. Bend the doubled end over to form a hook that will fit into the last loop on the other side of the necklace.

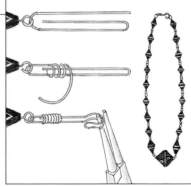

Tuareg Cross

For many years the Tuareg and Moors held sway over a significant area of North Africa. Now several tribes of nomadic Tuareg dwell in the Sahel, a belt of land spanning six countries south of the Sahara. Many have a specialized cross worn only by that tribe and named after its place of origin. This one, from Agadez in Niger, is undoubtedly the best known. Traditionally handed down from father to son as a talisman against the Evil Eye, these are now more often worn by women. Tuareg silverwork is characterized by the repeating geometric patterns which were thought to protect the wearer against the forces of bad magic. Early Tuareg crosses were made of Moroccan silver, later examples from imported European metal. Silver, believed to be blessed by the Prophet, was held more valuable than gold, the metal of the devil.

Above A Tuareg woman wearing her dowry jewelry. It can be bartered for livestock, food, or clothing.

Materials

1 silver Tuareg cross,
   3½ inches

6 Tuareg silver tubes, ¾ inch

14 flat silver beads, ⅛ inch

approximately 300 black
   rocailles, ⅛ inch

2 silver jumprings

1 silver S-clasp

2½ yards black linen or
   strong polycotton thread

beading needle

round-nosed pliers

*Total length excluding
   cross: 36 inches*

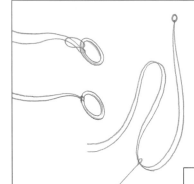

1 Double the thread and pass the folded end through one of the jumprings. Feed the cut ends through the loop and pull them tight to secure the jumpring to the thread. Thread on the needle and 12 inches of black rocailles.

2 Thread on 1 silver bead, 1 rocaille, 1 tube, 1 rocaille, 1 silver bead, 11 rocailles, 1 silver bead, 1 rocaille, 1 tube, 1 rocaille, 1 silver bead, 9 rocailles, 1 silver bead, 1 rocaille, 1 tube, 1 rocaille, 1 silver bead, 3 rocailles, 1 silver bead, 1 rocaille, and the cross.

3 Reverse the bead sequence to thread the other side of the necklace. Thread on the other jumpring and secure it by making an overhand knot as close to the last bead as possible. Then thread the needle back through the last 5 beads for a neat finish.

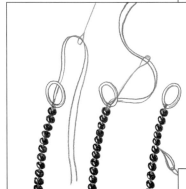

4 Remove the needle and knot the ends around the main strand. Dab a tiny drop of glue onto the knot and let it dry before cutting off the ends. Finally, use pliers to attach the S-clasp to one of the jumprings.

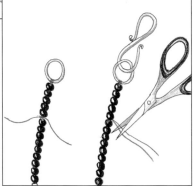

Ancient and Modern Egypt

A ncient Egypt grew up in the cultivated valley of the River Nile, which served as the lifeblood of the land. Each year the spring rains and the melting snow would cause it to flood, depositing onto the plains rich alluvia carried down from the heart of Africa by the Blue Nile and the White Nile. Cultivated land stretched only a few miles on each side of the Nile, so the inhabited land was a thin strip between the desert to the east and west, and the major highway was the river itself.

The jewelry and craftsmanship of the ancient Egyptian civilization, which extended from 3100 to 332 B.C. through 31 dynasties, are some of the most exquisite ever created. Materials such as lapis lazuli, turquoise, gold, jasper, and other semiprecious stones were already known and worked. Techniques and processes, some of which are still practiced, were first discovered, then improved, adapted, and developed during that 3,000-year span.

Near Luxor, where a great temple to the sun-god, Amen-Ra, was built during the eighteenth dynasty, lies the small village of Qorna where

Above Ancient faience found in a tomb (top), made from quartz sand, and modern ceramic faience beads (below).
Above right A wall painting found in the tomb of Sobkhotpe from the eighteenth dynasty, 1375 B.C., in Thebes, showing beadmaking. The long sticks are bow drills for making holes in the beads.
Left Handmade modern faience beads from Qorna bought in Luxor.
Right Enduring symbols of Egypt, the pyramids, including the great pyramid of Cheops, in the desert at Giza, outside Cairo.

about 25 families still make faience beads in a manner that would have been very familiar to the temple builders of 2,500 years ago.

Faience paste is made of clay, then dyed with earthy colors and wrapped around reeds to form tube beads. They are then cut into small sections with a razor blade and spread out on tables in the sun to dry. The reed that forms the central hole is then removed. The subtly colored beads are laid out on metal trays and baked over a fire fueled by dried cowdung. The understated beads can then be used to construct complicated and elaborate designs, such as those depicted on many of the ancient Egyptian friezes.

This is a simple form of beadmaking and makes use of natural materials found locally without any form of developed technology to facilitate the operation. It is as near to the basic

techniques used by ancient man as any we have seen, and is an art form that has survived the test of time over many centuries.

Filigree Work

Egypt was at the heart of trade routes that connected Africa to Europe and India, and thus became a center for innovation in the craft and technology of beadmaking. Filigree-work is a jewelry-making tradition that still thrives. Derived from the traditions of Islamic art, which forbids the representation of living creatures and exalts the ideal of balancing abstract geometry with flowing organic forms, filigree work incorporates abstract shapes such as lines, circles, spirals, and arabesques, along with granulation, in which tiny dots of metal are worked into the surface.

Much of the jewelry made in this way was created by Jewish artisans who had a virtual monopoly on the craft of the metalworker, one that they exploited for centuries.

Silver and gold were ideal for this style of work, and the wearing of such jewelry was a sign of a family's wealth. For many centuries, Egyptian brides have gone to their weddings decked out in a wonderful array of finely crafted filigree dowry jewelry.

Above Traditional hand-made faience beads.
Right Egyptian Islamic-era filigree necklace of large silver beads interspersed with long tubes. Coins and chains create an eye-catching centerpiece.

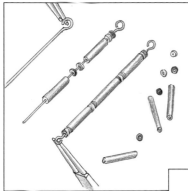

1 First make the 80 bars. Cut 80 pieces of wire 4 inches long and use round-nosed pliers to turn a loop at one end of each (see page 49). Thread on 2 ceramic beads, followed by 1 faience tube, 2 beads, 1 tube, 2 beads, 1 tube, and 2 beads. To complete each bar, turn a loop in the other end of the wire.

Faience Collar

This is a replica of the collar-style necklaces worn during the thousands of years of the ancient Egyptian dynasties. Produced from earlier than 3000 B.C., Egyptian faience was colored with a turquoise, green, or blue mixture.

These wide, elaborate collars, which were worn by ordinary men and women as well as by the Pharaohs, high priests, and officials, can be seen in ancient Egyptian tomb paintings, and carved into reliefs on temple walls.

Wealthy people may have mixed faience with precious and semiprecious stones and gold, while more humble citizens would have used faience to simulate stones and metal components.

2 For the inside row, cut 5½ feet of thread and double it. Pass the folded end through the split ring, feed the cut ends through the loop, and pull them tight to secure the ring to the thread. Attach the needle and thread on 3¾ inches of beads. Add one of the bars, passing the needle through the loop, then add 3 beads. Thread on all the bars, interspersing each with 2 or 3 beads. End the row with 4¾ inches of beads. Knot the ends securely to the hook.

Materials

approximately 1,500 cream, yellow, turquoise, brown, and terra-cotta ceramic beads, ⅒ inch

240 green ceramic clay tubes, approximately ½ inch

79 pairs of metal lotus shapes

6½ yards thread

4 yards of fine wire

1 hook and split ring

beading needle

clear glue

round-nosed pliers

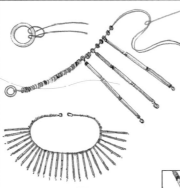

3 For the middle row, cut 6¼ feet of thread and double it. Tie one end neatly and securely around the inside row, ¾ inch from the first bar. Thread on 2 inches of beads, then pass the needle through the bottom loop of the first bar. Add 2 beads, then pass the needle through the top rings of 2 lotus shapes cupped together, followed by another 1 or 2 small beads. Repeat this sequence until you have incorporated all the bars, then thread on 2 inches of beads. Tie the ends neatly and firmly around the inside row, ¾ inch from the last bar.

Total length: 22 inches

(inside row)

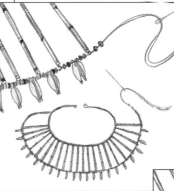

5 (Right) End the row with 2¼ inches of beads. Tie the loose ends around the inside row, 1½ inches from the last bar. Finally, secure all the knots with a small drop of glue, let it dry, then cut off the loose ends.

4 (Below) For the bottom row, cut 6¾ feet of thread and double it. Tie one end neatly and securely around the inside row, 1½ inches from the first bar. Thread on 2¼ inches of beads, then pass the needle through the bottom rings of the pairs of lotus shapes, interspersing each with 4 or 5 small beads.

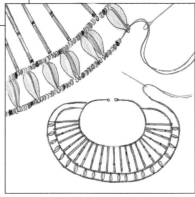

Horn of Africa

Christian Ethiopians of the highlands, isolated in their strongholds, have held fast to their religion since A.D. 4 and have survived many holy wars with Islamic invaders. One symbol typical of the region is the Ethiopian cross, worn as a neck pendant in a proud declaration of faith. Each area had its own design, named after a town or province, so it was possible to recognize where someone came from by the cross they wore. There are many variations representing peace, eternity, the Star of David, and the Maltese cross, either cut from the silver Maria Theresa dollars brought in by traders or fashioned by the lost-wax casting method.

Designs typical of other Ethiopian groups are both the triangular and crescent-shaped pendants, believed to offer protection against the Evil Eye and the power of the crescent moon. The breast motif, a powerful symbol of fertility, found widely across the continent, is also much in evidence.

On the coast of Africa, across the narrow strait that divides it from the extreme southwestern tip of Arabia, the influence of the highly skilled Yemeni silversmiths is clear in the elaborate gold and silverwork typical of the region. The Arab heritage is at its most apparent in the elaborate Islamic-style jewelry of the veiled nomad tribes from the deserts of North Africa.

Amber was brought in along the ancient trading routes to Egypt and hence south to the Horn of Africa. The Somalis are particularly enamored of amber, which is thought to have powerful healing properties, including protection against the Evil Eye, chills, and disease. Muslim tribespeople of the area have, for many centuries, fashioned the amber into beads that are then strung into prayer necklaces. Heavy dowry necklaces are formed from massive chunks of amber or copal, which are strung together in great lengths and worn by the bride at her wedding ceremony.

Above Oromo *Telsum* pendant, Welo Province. Triangles and crescents protect from the Evil Eye.
Right An Oromo woman at Senbete market with necklaces of silver breast motif beads, coral and glass beads, and silver Maria Theresa dollars.
Below Oromo silverwork.

Copal, like amber, is ancient tree resin. It is found in Korea, Zanzibar, and around the Tanzanian coast, rather than the Baltic. It is thought to be "young" amber, and is around 30,000 years old, compared with  amber's 40-million-year-old pedigree. Copal is admired by many African tribes, including the Somalis and the Berbers, both of whom use it extensively in their jewelry.

Buying Amber and Copal

Beware of plastic and synthetic copal look-alikes. Unfortunately much of what is passed off as real copal is imitation, so it is wise to be cautious. Simulated copal is often used, and much of the typical jewelry found in Africa nowadays contains plastic rather than the real thing. Like amber, copal generates electricity, and if you rub it very hard with your finger until it is hot you should, for a few seconds, be able to smell a fragrance reminiscent of honey and lemons. However, fake copal can be very pleasing and as long as you are not paying a copal price and you like it, buy it.

Above An Harari woman carries an *agelgil*, a type of basket, on her head. Around her neck she wears an amber necklace and a silver chain with a holder containing Koranic verses.

Right A valuable Somali necklace made of silver and amber, the latter of which is prized for its color, size, and magical healing properties. This piece forms part of a bride's dowry.

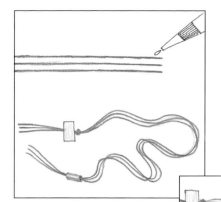

1 Either lay out the beads to determine stringing order or select them at random. Stiffen about 1 inch of one end of each strand of thread with glue (see Hint) and let it dry. Tie the other ends together with a loose knot and tape to the work surface.

Ethiopian Necklace of Silver and Glass

An example of ethnic craftsmanship at its most evocative, these large Ethiopian silver beads are a variation of the breast-shape motif, a symbol of fertility, which is popular in many parts of Africa. The red, orange, and yellow glass beads that make up the three-stranded sides are irregular in color and form, and the fact that the artisan has not strictly stuck to his pattern adds to the haphazard charm of the piece.

It is easy to imagine him sitting with piles of colored beads in front of him, absentmindedly selecting and stringing them.

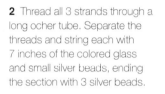

2 Thread all 3 strands through a long ocher tube. Separate the threads and string each with 7 inches of the colored glass and small silver beads, ending the section with 3 silver beads.

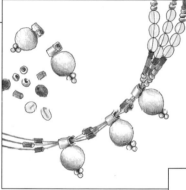

Materials

13 Ethiopian round silver
   beads, approximately
   1 inch

2 ocher glass tubes, ¾ inch

6 red glass ovals, ⅜ inch

15 red glass ovals, ⅜ inch

33 yellow glass ovals, ³⁄₁₆ inch

100 glass tubes, in red, ocher,
   and orange, ¼ inch

78 silver beads, ⅛ inch

2 black glass beads, ³⁄₁₆ inch

3 yards twisted cord thread,
   cut into 3 equal lengths

clear glue

masking tape

Total length excluding tassel:
   26 inches

3 Pass the 3 threads together through a large round silver bead. Separate the threads and add 1 glass tube to each. Repeat this process, separating and joining the threads, until you have used up all the large silver beads. Then make the second side of the necklace, threading the remaining smaller beads onto the 3 separate strands.

Hint

As the thread is very thick, rather than using a needle, stiffen the end with clear glue or gum arabic, which means you can push it through the beads. Squeeze a little glue onto scrap paper and pull the end of the thread through it, twisting as you do so, until it is thinly coated.

4 Thread the 3 strands through the second long ocher tube. Untape and untie the other end, then pass all 6 strands through the 2 black glass beads which can be moved up and down to act as shorteners. Tie all strands together with an overhand knot about 1 inch from the tubes. Trim off the glued ends, leaving a tassel of about 7½ inches

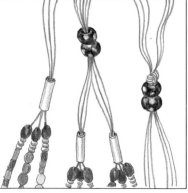

The Masai

The Masai are a pastoral, nomadic tribe living in parts of Kenya and Tanzania. Renowned for their exceptional physique, the warriors adorn their bodies with jewelry, scars, and decorations such as ostrich-feather plumes, monkey-skin anklets, and lions' mane headdresses as a sign of their achievements and great courage. From the early eighteenth century, the women made jewelry from brightly colored European beads traded into Africa.

The Masai people have kept their traditions with fierce pride, maintaining a hierarchy in which young warriors progress through age-sets until they become elders at thirty. This marks the end of their most enjoyable years and is celebrated with a magnificent ceremony that lasts for up to five days and culminates in the shaving of their heads. The warriors, with their chalk-painted bodies adorned with beaded gifts from their mothers and girlfriends, together with other trappings of their success as warriors, display their skill and grace in a ritual dance. The women of the Masai tribe also wear fine beadwork, which signifies their rank, clan, and skills.

Above Decorations like those worn by this Kenyan Masai woman indicate her clan and social status.

Below Colorful beaded collars, a typical form of adornment, displayed on a Kenyan market stall.

Above Long beaded ear-lobe pendants are worn only by married women, who should never be seen by their husbands without them. Their heads are shaved to emphasize their colorful jewelry.

Left Elaborate beaded collars are traditionally worn during Masai marriage ceremonies.
Right An antique collar made with strands of different-colored opaque glass beads, further ornamented with coins.

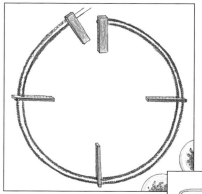

1 Cut the leather to make 3 spacers of ¼ x 2 inches and 2 of ⅛ x 2 inches. Using an awl, pierce 12 evenly spaced holes through the ⅛ inch thickness of each spacer. Starting with the outside row, cut a piece of wire 5 feet long, bend it in half, and thread a cut end through the outer hole of a ¼ x 2 inch spacer, then thread the other cut end

Masai Collar

This colorful twelve-row Masai collar is similar to those worn by the women of the tribe. Sometimes many collars are worn at once, together with other decorations such as beaded snuff boxes and earlobe pendants. The color of each bead has its own meaning: the blue beads signify God and the sky, and the green beads symbolize vegetation and are a sign of peace. The necklace is challenging to make, and just as the Masai work with the few basic materials available to them, you will need patience and ingenuity to fashion your own leather spacers and metal fastening. Try to find some old, irregular rocailles or bugles to give character to the piece.

through the adjacent hole. Push the spacer down to the end loop in the wire; this will be at 12 o'clock on the collar. Thread approximately 7 inches of beads onto the outside wire until you reach the 3 o'clock point of the circle. Pass the wire through the outer hole of a ⅛ inch spacer. Add a further 7 inches of beads, then the ¼ inch spacer at 6 o'clock, and so on until you reach the third ¼ inch spacer at 12 o'clock. Repeat with the inner section of wire. Do not finish off the ends until the collar is completed in case you need to alter something.

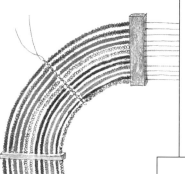

2 Cut a piece of wire 4⅞ feet long, bend it in half, and thread with beads as before. Cut 3¼ inches of wire and use pliers to shape it into a hook. Bend the cut ends so that they will hook under the fifth and sixth end loops of the doubled wire to hold the clasp in place against the first 12 o'clock spacer.

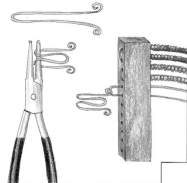

3 Thread 4 further doubled wire lengths in the same way as the first 2 until the basic necklace structure is completed. Halfway between each spacer, wind one end of a piece of wire, approximately 6 inches long, around the outside row. Then loop it around each subsequent row of beads, finishing off on the inside row with a neat loop.

Materials

4 ozs. red, green, white, blue, orange, and striped bugles and rocailles, ⅛ inch

leather (¾ x 2 x ⅛ inch thick) for 5 spacers; alternatively buy 12-hole metal or bone spacers

11 yards of very fine springy silver-plated wire

7 oval beads, ¼ inch, for decorating spacers (optional)

awl

needle-nose pliers

wire cutters

Total length:
outside row, 29 inches;
inside row 18 inches

4 Twist the pairs of loose ends together securely and cut off the ends of the 2 outer and 2 inner pairs. To make the other side of the clasp, cut a piece of wire about 2½ inches long and bend the cut ends to form loops. Wind the remaining loose ends securely around the loops, then cut off the ends neatly.

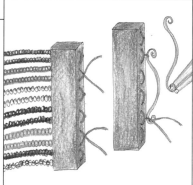

63

African Cowrie Shell and Rocaille Earrings

These earrings are made by Kenya's Masai tribe, using the cowrie shell, an important symbol of fertility, and blue beads that represent the sky. Cowrie shells are important in many parts of the world, even being used as currency. Cowries are often sold in markets and bead shops with the backs sliced off so the beads will sit better. These earrings are not difficult to make provided you are patient with your threading.

Materials

2 cowrie shell beads, ¾ inch	15 feet of very fine wire
2 blue rocailles, ⅛ inch	ear hooks
approximately 600 blue rocailles, ¹⁄₁₆ inch	round-nosed pliers
	wire cutters

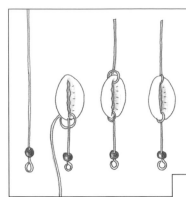

1 Cut a length of wire 7 inches long and use pliers to turn a small loop at one end (see page 49). Thread a large rocaille onto the wire. Place the shell ½ inch above it and loop the wire 2–3 times around one end to secure it. Pass the wire up through the shell and secure it at the top in the same way.

2 Cut a 22-inch length of wire. Wrap one end tightly around the wire protruding from the top of the shell and cut off the excess with wire cutters. Thread on enough small blue rocailles to frame one side of the cowrie shell (about 20) and curve the

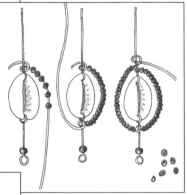

wire to frame the shell snugly. Loop the wire around the wire stem at the bottom of the shell. Thread more blue rocailles onto the wire to frame the other side of the shell. Loop the wire around the stem at the top of the shell above the first loop.

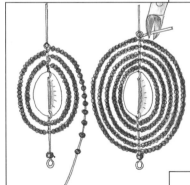

3 Repeat the beading until you have 5 rows on each side. Wind the wire tightly around the stem and cut off any excess.

4 Cut the wire stem to ¼ inch and bend to form a loop for the ear hook. Thread the loop through the ear hook and close the loop. Twist the stem so that the earring hangs properly.

Ndebele Beadwork

The Ndebele people live near the border of South Africa and Zimbabwe and are closely related to the Zulus. The women are famed for the heavy brass rings they wear around their necks and legs, symbols of their married status and worn with pride even though they hinder movement and can eventually cause damage to the spine.

The Ndebele are also known for their bead embroidery on aprons, headdresses, and cloaks. Rocailles are sewn onto beaten goatskin or canvas in a variety of intricate patterns, echoing the traditional geometric designs on the painted walls of their houses.

White is predominant, but other colors—reds, greens, blues, and black—also feature strongly. The women also wear thick collars of twisted grasses encrusted with seed beads, known as *rholwani*, often worn in combination with beaded bracelets and arm bands. Similar beaded designs are often incorporated into the men's ceremonial battledress.

Below A Ndebele woman wearing traditional dress including brass collars and fine beadwork.

Right An elaborately beaded Ndebele collar.

Below Ndebele women creating traditional beadwork, with designs similar to their vividly decorated houses, seen here.

Zulu Beadwork

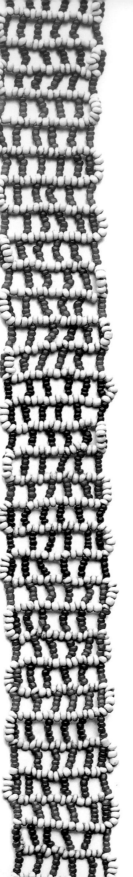

Along the northeastern coast of South Africa lies the kingdom of the Zulus, formed in the early part of the nineteenth century by their powerful leader, Shaka. With a mixture of political astuteness and military discipline, he forged a unified nation from the disparate tribes of the region as a response to the encroachment of European colonialism.

The nineteenth century saw a steady influx of trade beads to the area, and Shaka was so great a bead lover that he decreed any new bead arriving in the country should immediately be shown to him so that he could decide whether he wanted to keep it for himself. They were not only considered objects of beauty, but became integral to Zulu society, denoting social status and achievements of the wearer, just as military uniforms denote rank and regiment. When Shaka's mother died, the wearing of beads was banned for a year as a sign of mourning.

The Zulus invented a whole language of beads, using them to send messages of love, devotion, and betrayal. Colors are invested with many symbolic meanings; white is the purity of love, black means the darkness of night, pink means poverty, while green

signifies coolness or fertility. Blue has various meanings, ranging from the sky's wide expanse to the callous spurning of a lover.

These messages are encoded into a huge variety of artifacts including bags, belts, collars, and headdresses. The traditional format for these "love letters," however, are the tab pendants that hang from necklaces made by the young women and offered as love tokens to the unmarried warriors of the tribe.

Far left Zulu woman chief with beaded ornaments.
Left and above Open beadwork belt (left) and beaded bag (above), worked in subtler colors than in modern pieces.

Right These Zulu collars are made from European rocailles, probably Czech or Venetian. They are filled with grass, covered with hide, then wrapped and stitched with bead strings.

Kenya: Batik Bone and Ostrich Shells

Bone beads with a batik-style pattern are some of the most spectacular modern beads to be found in Africa. Most are made in Kenya, and they tend to be large and round, although tubes and smaller round beads are also made. Only the large bones from cattle and oxen are dense enough to make these beads. The stark geometric patterns are very striking, reminiscent of the African art that had such a profound impact on the art of twentieth-century Europe. Necklaces made of these beads, as well as individual beads, have become widely available around the world.

After boiling in large cauldrons, the bones are then laid out to dry, bleached, cut into strips, and then into bead-sized chunks. Wooden plugs, drilled with a hole, are inserted into the cavity of the bone to help the beads hang straight. The chunks are then polished on lathes, creating a smooth surface to receive the batiking wax. After applying wax in patterns, the beads are heated in vats of black dye so the exposed parts are stained black and the areas covered with wax remain white. When dry, the hardened wax is removed by picking or scraping gently against the bone, revealing the white

Above from top A hollow bone is cut to size, then a wooden plug inserted. Batiking wax is then applied in striking patterns. The beads are dyed, then the wax carefully removed to reveal the undyed white pattern underneath.
Right Carved cow bone beads made by the Kipsigis tribe near Nairobi.

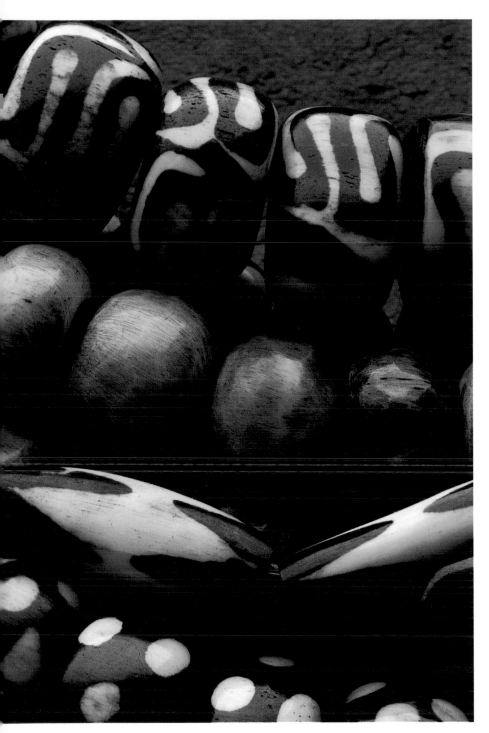

patterns underneath. All the wax is cleaned off, then the beads are gently buffed until highly polished before being strung together.

Ostrich Shell Beads

A traditional bead-making material used for over 9,000 years in Kenya is the ostrich egg shell. The shells are cut into rough blanks, then drilled. They are threaded onto strings and then smoothed on a stone or against a buffing wheel. A similar process is used in many parts of the world, for instance, in making heishi beads in America and coco beads in the Philippines. These shells are used in many ways: as single-strand necklaces, woven into aprons, or as the multistrand belt shown above.

Above A Turkana woman wearing a belt made of strings of ostrich shell discs over a skirt of soft leather. This costume, including an elaborate bead pendant necklace, is worn by the young women of the tribe to indicate that they are ready for marriage.

Right Ostrich shell disc beads are made by cutting rough shapes from the shell, piercing and stringing them, then smoothing the edges on a stone or wheel.

Ghana: Recycled Glass Beadmaking

In West Africa, the multicolored millefiori trade beads are sliced into tiny disks, and glass beads from many sources are rubbed against stones to change their appearance, ground into new shapes, or heated to create a new art form.

The Krobos and Asantes from Ghana have their own style of beadmaking—a fusion of ancient and modern, following those techniques first used in ancient Egypt from as early as 1800 B.C. They also use modern materials such as broken glass bottles, crushed and ground into fine powder with a pestle and mortar, then made into beads. One of the best-known beadmakers in the village of Odumase is Mohammed Cedi, who makes the big, zigzag striped *bodom* beads—*bodom* means "to bark" in the local dialect. He starts

Above A Krobo woman from Ghana wearing an assortment of locally made recycled glass beads in typical colors.

Right Recycled glass beads interspersed with rocailles, silver, and copal. The bicones are copies of early Victorian trade beads.

off by pounding clear scrap glass into small pieces, which he then grinds to a fine powder on a grinding stone before adding pigments or ground glass to color the bead.

A bead mold, made of clay, is dipped in kaolin so the beads can be easily removed. A cassava leaf stem is placed in the middle of the mold, which will burn out to form a perfectly shaped hole when the bead is fired. The first layer of white powdered glass is poured into the mold and the edges are defined with a thin stick, producing a sharp line separating the different colors. Black powdered glass is poured on top of the white in a zigzag pattern, then more white powder is added. In the middle or "belly" of the bead, brown "eyes" are sprinkled between the zigzags, then the whole process is repeated in reverse to make a symmetrical design. The mold is tapped gently on the table to settle the powder.

The beads are fired in dome-shaped clay kilns that have an opening at the back for the firewood and a door at the front through which the artisan can check on the molds. The firing time depends on the type of bead being made. Plain opaque beads take 20 to 40 minutes, and *bodom* beads between 45 and 90 minutes. As the glass powder heats in the kiln, it becomes viscous and sinters together to form a bead. During the firing a wooden-handled metal pin is inserted into the holes and the beads are dislodged in the mold to see if they have set. When they are ready, the metal pin is inserted again, and the beads are pressed hard against the side of the mold to shape them into the round, bicone, and barrel bead shapes typical of this style of beadmaking.

An alternative production method uses glass bottles smashed into large shards and then placed in the mold. When fired, the glass melts to produce a more translucent effect, especially when several colors are used, perhaps from dark brown or dark green beer bottles. Holes are pierced in the beads while the glass is still very hot. The beads are polished on a grinder to bring out the luster, rubbed in sand, and given a final polish with machine oil.

Above Necklaces made from a typical range of Ghanaian glass beads, showing how the layers of powdered glass have been placed to create patterns. The colors and patterns were inspired by those of Venetian trade beads, as seen on page 21.

Right from top The main stages in the manufacture of recycled glass beads. Finely powdered colored glass is carefully added to the molds layer by layer to achieve the desired design. The beads are then fired in a dome-shaped kiln.

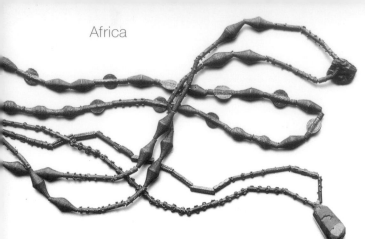

Lost-Wax Method

The lost-wax method of working metals such as gold or brass has been used by many unconnected cultures scattered around the world. Particularly striking examples of beads and other decorative items made in this way have been found as far afield as the Peruvian Andes, Egypt, and India's Gangetic Plain.

The traditional metalworkers of Ghana and the Ivory Coast, including the Asante and the Baoule, still use this traditional technique to form a variety of objects and beads astounding both for their beauty of craftsmanship and the sheer size and weight of the pieces.

Perhaps unsurprisingly, much of the gold jewelry made in this time-consuming way was owned by the nobility. In fact, so heavy and ornate was the jewelry of one king of the Asante tribe that a small boy walked slowly beside him so that his gold-bedecked arms could rest on the boy's head.

Although there are several methods of lost-wax casting, the most common technique is to model the item first in wax. When the artisan has finished the wax model, it is dipped into a very thin liquid clay (a slip) and a thick layer of clay is then added, encasing the model. A small

Left The brass beads in these old necklaces were modeled first in wax, then cast in brass, using the lost-wax technique. The beads were made by the Baoule people of the Ivory Coast.
Below Contemporary lost wax brass beads, also from the Ivory Coast, strung together with European glass beads, found in a market in Accra, Ghana.

tube of wax is left pointing through the clay, forming a hole. The clay covering, known as an "investment", is baked hard and the wax melts and runs out through the hole.

Molten metal is then poured into the hollow clay mold. When the metal has cooled, the "investment" is broken to reveal the metal object inside, which is then polished to a shine.

This is an incredibly painstaking and time-consuming process of metal casting because each finished bead will be an exact replica of its wax model. In this process, the clay mold is destroyed every time, and each bead must be created with a new model and a new mold.

Bida Glassmakers

Bida, in Nigeria, is the capital of the ancient kingdom of the Nupe, an Islamic tribe that has become renowned for its outstanding glasswork. Although many of the African cultures once made glass beads in the traditional way, Bida is now the only place in Africa where this method of working glass is still practiced, using techniques that have been passed down through the centuries. It is even possible that these methods first came to Africa from the countries of the Middle East for the glassworkers of Hebron still make their glass bracelets in the same way as the craftsmen of Bida. Perhaps this is not as surprising as it might seem since the Nupe believe they originally came from Egypt.

In this traditional manufacturing process, quartz sand, chalk, and natron from Lake Chad are heated for hours in a furnace. The end result is a dark brown molten mass that is almost completely clear when it is held up to the light. The molten glass is then wound around iron rods to produce the characteristic beads and bracelets in dark browns and greens, which are often overlaid with white or yellow lines and little glass snakes.

Above Nupe bead sellers showing their wares in the market in Bida, Nigeria. Bida glass is also widely traded to other tribes.
Right A necklace of beads made from recycled glass.
Below The constituents of glass being melted in a traditional Bida furnace before the beadmaking process begins.

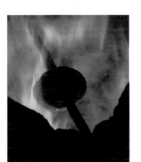
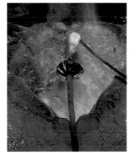
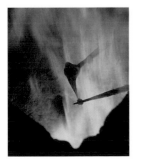

The Indian
Subcontinent

AFGHANISTAN

Kabul

Islamabad

Afghan
Silverwork

Afghan
Lapis Lazuli

PAKISTAN

Pakistani Silver

Karachi

INDUS

RAJASTHAN

Ceramic

Jaipur

Bone

Rajasthani
Silver

GUJARAT

GULF OF
KHAMBHAT

Bombay

Pane

ARABIAN
SEA

Cambay
Carved Cornelian

Goa

Ceramic

DECCAN

KRISHNA

NILGIRI
HILLS

Ootacamund

KERALA

Cochin

CAPE COMORIN

HINDU-KUSH

KARAKORUM

Kashmiri Metal, with
Turquoise and Coral

KASHMIR

Bone

Silver
Delhi

Ceramic

GANGES

Soapstone

YAMUNA

Lac

Ivory

Glass

Varanasi

INDIA

Ceramic

GODAWARI

Hyderabad

Glass

Glass

Madras

RAMESWARAM

SRI LANKA

CHINA

TIBET

Peach
Stone

Lhasa

Silver

NEPAL

▲ EVEREST

SIKKIM

Feather Glass

BHUTAN

BRAHMAPUTRA

NAGALAND

Mizoram
Pumtek

Carved Wood

Calcutta

BANGLADESH

Dhaka

MIZORAM

BURMA
(MYANMAR)

ORISSA

Wood and Inlay

Amethyst

Naga
Shell

Decorated
Wood

BAY OF BENGAL

The Indian subcontinent takes its name from the Indus, one of the two mighty rivers of the region. The Indus Valley in Pakistan was the site of one of the world's first great civilizations, and one to which the origins of the Hindu religion and modern Indian culture can be traced. Enriching influences from East and West are also much in evidence. Many of the people have a passion for self-adornment, as strong today as in the past. Jewelry is worn extensively by all classes and at all times, and beads and beadwork are an essential ingredient in Indian dress.

They not only beautify the wearer, but also serve as a tangible show of wealth or provide protection in the form of a talisman. Some precious and semiprecious stones are thought to hold magical or medicinal properties to protect the wearer against illness or misfortune.

Throughout the subcontinent, from Tibet and Nepal to Sri Lanka, from Afghanistan to Bangladesh, craftspeople, working with very basic tools, continue age-old traditions and skills using a great variety of materials and methods. Beads of natural materials such as seeds and nuts are simply threaded onto strings. Fragrant wood such as sandalwood and the stems of the sacred basil plant (*tulsi*) are turned and strung into necklaces. Wooden beads are decorated with traditional Indian designs

Previous pages Clockwise from left: turquoise from Tibet; amber and silver from Mizoram; heavy Indian silver and gilded silver; Naga necklace; Varanasi ceramic beads.
Above A woman from Pushkar in Rajasthan, wearing jewelry that forms both her dowry and her family's wealth.
Left Singers from Kinnaur in Kashmir, wearing traditional turquoise and coral beads typical of many Himalayan groups.
Right Ghats (steps) in the holy city of Varanasi, where pilgrims bathe in the sacred waters of the River Ganges. Necklaces (*malas*) of beads or blossoms are an important component of the Hindu religion.

and images. Skilled artists dexterously paint birds, animals, flowers, and exotic designs onto wooden spheres to create exquisite beads.

Areas noted for fine wood-carving and painting include the state of Rajasthan and the holy city of Varanasi, which have strong craft traditions. Animal products such as bone and horn are turned, then carved intricately into objects of great beauty. Glass beadmaking in India is also very highly developed, especially in Purdalpur, Firozabad, and Varanasi. Soapstone, soft and easily worked, is also carved into beads. Mines in the eastern state of Orissa produce garnet and amethyst. These, as well as other semiprecious stones such as agate and cornelian, are made into distinctive shapes, both here and in the western state of Gujarat— a source of beads that has dominated much of the world market for 5,000 years.

Indian Glass Beads

Glass beadmaking in India has been a huge industry for thousands of years. Most Indian glass beads are blown, drawn or wound. The latter are wound in furnaces (furnace wound) or formed over lamps (lamp wound).

Furnace Beads

Glass is made in several centers around India, but no other village has quite as strong a bead economy as Purdalpur near Agra. With over a hundred factories, it is renowned in the bead world. We visited a small workshop with simple walls of wattle and a straw roof to see a round glass furnace made of clay, with fifteen glowing work stations. In front of each one, a glassworker sat crosslegged before his crucible. Different activities take place at the same furnace, simple canes are drawn, and beads are wound around long iron rods or mandrels.

As we watched, a glassmaker drew two long rods from his crucible, with a mass of molten glass adhering to the ends. He handed one of the rods to a young lad, who walked slowly up the dusty lane, pulling the molten glass

Above Indian glass beads, including wound glass beads with spiral trails (the small one formed in a mold), and more wound glass beads with metalic aventurine decoration.

into a thin cane that cooled as he walked. This was broken into short lengths, sorted with other colors, then placed in bundles on a piece of cardboard.

A second worker was taking up the colorful bundles, setting them in a circle on a spade-like tool. The man inserted them into his fiery workstation, then withdrew them and hammered the now-molten glass with a flat tool, forming wheel shapes. As we picked our way around the crowded furnace, we watched other processes. Round beads were being wound onto iron rods, then shaped while still molten, glass bangles were expertly formed onto metal cones, then dropped into annealing pots and allowed to cool slowly.

Purdalpur bazaar was a hive of beadmaking activity. Multicolored beads could be seen at almost every stall, being counted, sorted, threaded, and packed, continuing an important tradition that is centuries old.

Lamp Beads

Lamp glass bead production is widespread in India. A simple gas lamp is used to produce the high temperatures required to melt the

From far left The wood-fired furnace at Purdalpur. A gather of molten glass is taken from the furnace on two rods and carried outside. The glassmaker's assistant takes one rod and walks down the alley, drawing out a cane of molten glass behind him.

glass canes. The flames in the furnace can be fanned higher by a foot-operated bellows set into the workbench.

Beadworkers first dip a copper rod into a slip (wet clay solution) so the bead can removed easily when it is finished. The rod is twisted swiftly in one hand and when the cane, held in the flames by the other hand, has become molten, it will be wound deftly around the rod. Skill and habit will guarantee that the correct amount of glass is wound around the rod, and a mold will be used to form a perfect shape.

Like an artist with an array of paintbrushes, the beadmaker might pick up a second cane of colored glass, heat it, and use it, for instance, to encircle the center of the bead. Tiny pinpricks of color from a contrasting colored cane will add detail, or he may add stripes, dots, whorls, or zigzags, using his artistic skill to produce personal design flourishes.

Many beads are made on one rod, and soon the work station is covered with bowls of canes and rods sticking up like hatpins. When the glass cools, the beads are eased off the rod, and as the china clay pulls away, it leaves a little dusting inside the hole of the bead, a good way of identifying these Indian-made lamp beads.

Above Bright wound glass beads string together with wire work.

Above right Making lamp beads: a molten glass cane is wound around a metal rod. A number of beads are made on each rod, left to cool, then slipped off the rod.

Right A necklace of glass rings and tubular glass beads, in the brilliant colors much-loved on the subcontinent. The rings are made in the same way as glass bangles.

Prayer Beads

The earliest known use of prayer beads was on a statue of a Hindu sage from the third century B.C. The main Hindu sects of modern times are the followers of Shiva, who use beads made of rudraksha nuts, and the followers of Vishnu, who carry beads made from the sacred basil, or *tulsi* plant.

Other prayer bead users include the Jains and Buddhists, two of the three great offshoots of Hinduism. Buddhism spread east to Southeast Asia, China, Japan, and Tibet. It was in Tibet that beads of human bone, particularly of high-ranking monks of lamas, were held in great reverence, as are beads of coral, amber, and wood from the sacred bo tree.

Islam is the other great religion of the subcontinent. Their rosary, thought to have been inspired by Buddhist examples, consists of ninety-nine beads representing the divine attributes of God, with the hundredth bead reserved for His name. This rosary, in its turn, inspired the Christian Catholic rosary.

Above Tibetan women making puja in Lhasa, the capital, with prayer bead of wood, turquoise, and coral placed on the ground beside them.

1 Using pliers, grip a 2-inch piece of wire ¾ inch from the bottom and make a loop by bending the bottom end upward and across the pliers. Hold the loop with pliers and twist the free end twice around the wire with your fingers, working downward. Snip off close to the loop.

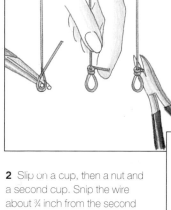

2 Slip on a cup, then a nut and a second cup. Snip the wire about ¾ inch from the second cup and make a second loop as before. Snip off the wire close to the loop.

Materials

54 drilled rudraksha nuts, other
    nuts, seeds or beads (about
    ½ inch diameter)

108 bead cups, to fit nuts

about 4 yards of fine wire
    cut into 2-inch lengths
    (see Hints)

round-nosed pliers

wire cutters

Total length: 3 feet

Rudraksha Nut Temple Necklace

Prayer bead necklaces and scented garlands of flowers (*malas*) are sold from the *malawallah* stalls inside Hindu temple complexes all over India. This example was bought from a vendor inside the enormous and ancient Menakshi temple in Madurai, Tamil Nadu, and is made of red-brown, knobbly, five-sided rudraksha nuts, known as "Shiva's eyes". The necklace is worked with the pinning technique with sophisticated metal cups placed on each side of the nut. It will take some time, but it is a useful technique and any kind of seed or bead can be used.

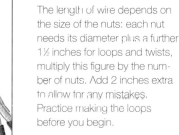

Hints

The length of wire depends on the size of the nuts: each nut needs its diameter plus a further 1½ inches for loops and twists, multiply this figure by the number of nuts. Add 2 inches extra to allow for any mistakes. Practice making the loops before you begin.

3 Take the next piece of wire, push it through the completed loop, then make the first loop of the next bead. Feed on cup, nut, and cup as before, followed by another loop. Repeat until 53 nuts have been used. Attach the final bead as shown, inserting the final loop through the last loops on each end of the necklace.

Bone and Horn Beads from Delhi

Bone has been used for ornamentation as long as man has been a hunter. Using the teeth, claws, tusks, quills, feathers, and bones from his quarry, he has created all manner of artistic adornments for himself, varying from headdresses, hats, caps, haircombs, earrings, and necklaces to bow quivers, waist belts, breast ornaments, skirts, cloaks, and shoes. Bone is a natural product, with a clean whiteness and smooth quality that can be easily carved and drilled, then dyed, so that an infinite variety of designs can be created, making it a most versatile and satisfying medium to work.

The kind of bone used can be a problem in India—Muslims may not touch pigs, while Hindus hold cattle sacred. Accordingly, much of the bone used is that of buffalo or camels, and any cattle bones must be prepared by non-Hindu craftsmen.

Only four main bones from each animal are large enough to be used in bead production. They are first sliced into strips about 6 inches long and ½ inch square, then cut into smaller pieces according to the size of bead required.

Above This beadmaker uses a handheld grinding tool to create the pattern on the bone bead.

The holes in the beads are made first, drilled from one end, then from the other so the holes meet in the middle.

Shaping is done at a grinding wheel. To make a round bead, the worker holds the bead on a stick with a metal point through the hole. He then holds the bead against the wheel for just long enough to round off the squared ends; then a selection of chisels is used to shape the ends. Patterns are applied using a small, hand-held grinding wheel and the craftsman has to

Left A beadmaking workshop on the outskirts of Delhi, specializing in making bone beads. The beads are cut to size, a hole is drilled, and then the beads are smoothed against a buffing wheel.

make sure he repeats the pattern perfectly each time for continuity and conformity. The bead is then immersed in soda for two hours.

Large drums full of beads are sprinkled with hydrogen peroxide, covered with water, and soaked for 24 hours until bleached white.

The beads are then colored, if required. The familiar brown shade is achieved by dipping in a brew of tea that is sometimes extremely strong! When dry, the beads are strung into lengths of 16 inches and polished against a buffing wheel to create uniformly smooth edges.

Last, they may be either unstrung or left on their strings, then checked at the main depot for quality and correct sizing.

Carvers can be extremely skilled, and many of them produce highly delicate work, clipping intricate filigree shapes out of drilled blank pieces of bone. Formerly, the finest ivory carving was done in the same way.

Left Intricately carved bone and horn beads, the latter carved in the style of earlier French beads.

Above Thatched houses on the outskirts of Delhi, where craftsmen and farmers work side by side.

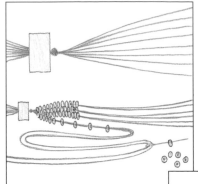

1 Measure the length you need for the belt and add on an extra 12 inches. Cut 8 pieces of linen thread this length, then tie them together in a loose overhand knot and tape it to the work surface. Divide the 8 strands into pairs and thread a beading needle onto each, then thread each of the 4 double strands with 10 bone disks.

2 Separate the strands and thread 2 bone disks onto each of the 8 strands. Insert each strand through the 8 holes of a 1¾ inch bone spacer and pull gently taut. For each strand of the main sections, thread on the following: 1 brass (or wooden) bead, 10–14 bone disks, 1 brass bead, 1 bone tube, 1 brass bead, 10–14 bone disks, 1 brass bead. (The bone disks vary in size, but the spacers should be equidistant.) Then thread on a 2-inch bone spacer. Repeat until you have 7 main sections, using the 2½-inch spacers next, then the second 2-inch spacer and the second 1¾-inch spacer.

Bone Bead Belt

This is a contemporary beaded belt, bought in London but inspired by complex Naga examples consisting of up to 40 strands, incorporating glass beads, bone spacers, and brass bells. This simple version uses small bone beads and bone tube inserts—some are dyed to represent coral. Small brass or wooden beads give detail, and the eight-hole bone spacers will help the belt keep its shape. The spacers divide the belt into seven 3-inch sections, though you can tailor it to your own size requirements, substituting wooden spacers and glass, coco, or wooden beads instead of bone. The belt's long tasseled ends are separate components – make them yourself, or buy them.

Materials

8 bone 8-row spacers,
  each ⅜ inch wide—
  2 of 1¾ inches,
  2 of 2 inches ,
  4 of 2½ inches
For the end sections:
120 white bone disks, ¼ inch
For each of the 7 sections:
32 brass or brown wooden
  beads, ⅛ inch
about 200 white bone discs,
  ¼ inch

8 thin white or coral-colored
  bone tubes, ⅜–½ inch
at least 17 yards linen thread
2 twisted cords with tassel
  ends, 16 inches long
1 yard silk thread, to match
  tassels
4 beading needles
darning needle
masking tape
clear glue
Beaded length: 27 inches

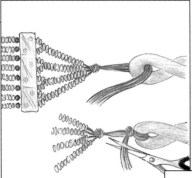

3 For the end section, thread 2 bone disks onto each of the 8 strands. Divide the strands into pairs and thread 10 bone disks onto each. Tie all 8 strands in an overhand knot close to the last bead. Pass the threads through the loop of the tasseled cord and tie a neat knot. Apply a small drop of glue and let it dry before cutting off the ends.

4 Hold one end of the silk thread along the length of the join and, beginning next to the last bead, wind it neatly over itself and around the join. When you reach the cord, secure the thread with a knot, then thread on the darning needle and push it through the whipping before cutting off the end. Attach the other end in the same way.

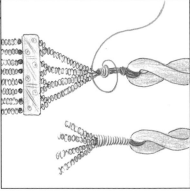

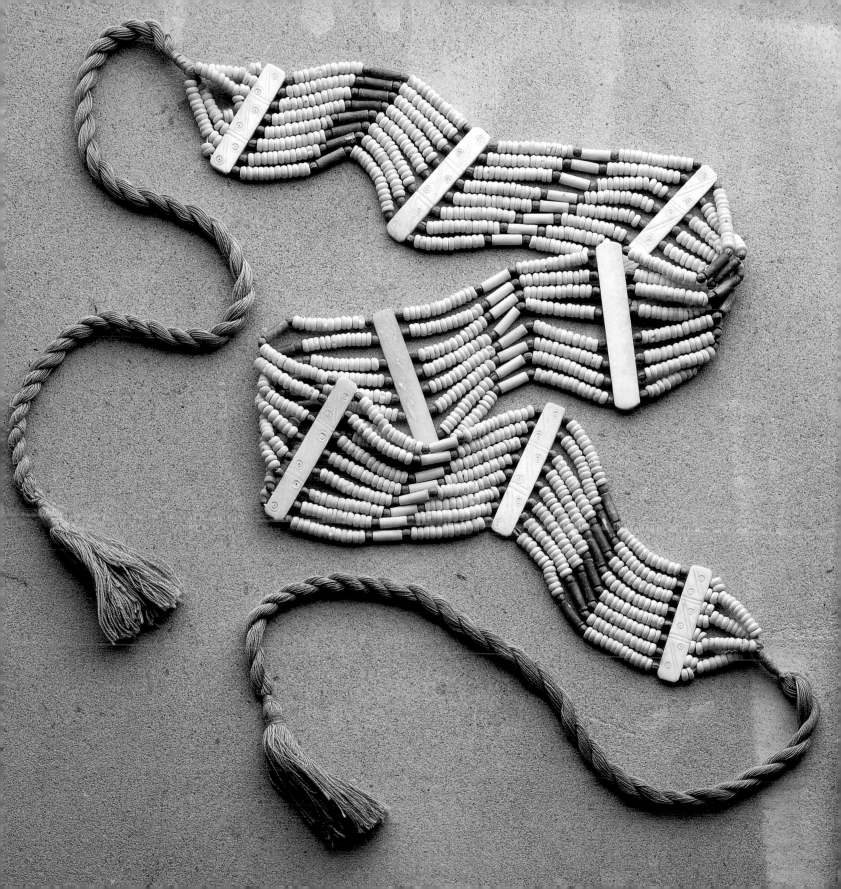

Nagaland

Nagaland is a small state in the northeast of India, high up in the foothills of the Himalaya, almost impossible to visit because of political insurrection, but its people and their culture, past and present, are of particular interest to collectors of bead jewelry.

Detective work by anthropologists suggests that the Nagas migrated from China and Southeast Asia, arriving in the area in about A.D. 1010. They live in Nagaland and over the border in Burma. By 1971, the official Indian census established the Naga population at just over half a million people, divided into 16 tribes living in separate villages. Some of those tribes are further linked into larger, stronger groups, almost like mini-states.

Over the centuries, the Naga people gained celebrity status and notoriety as a result of their headhunting traditions. Marauding parties swooped down on other villages, not for territorial reasons, but solely to gather heads. A man with many heads to his credit gained higher status, and carved wooden heads were a distinctive element of Naga decoration.

The Nagas' esthetic sense and imagination is demonstrated in other distinctive personal

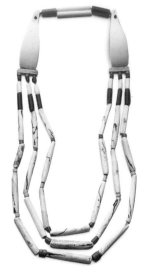

Above Naga necklace of conch shell tubes, separated by smaller cornelian beads, with bone spacers and sections of conch shells that lie over the shoulders, allowing the beads to hang evenly.
Below Shell necklaces like this often include cornelian or glass beads, conch shell clasps, and can be either single strand or multistrand.

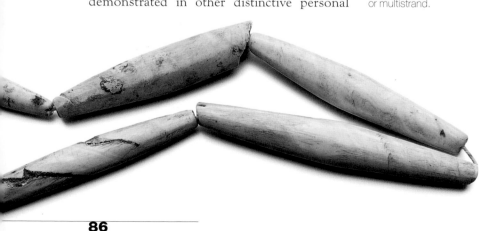

adornments. Using natural materials such as shells (especially cowrie and conch shells), ivory, boar's tusks, tiger teeth, feathers, and claws, as well as rock crystal, cornelian, trade beads, and other materials, they produced outstandingly beautiful necklaces, belts, skirts, armlets, wristlets, leggings, headdresses, chest ornaments, and ear ornaments.

Some metal was also used, and fluted brass beads, like small trumpets, are sometimes included in necklaces. Bead belts with bone spacers, such as the project on page 84, were traditional garb for women, and the bead necklaces shown here and in the project on the following page are also typical.

The decline of Naga traditions, especially the taking of heads, began under the British Raj and was hastened as a result of the efforts of Christian missionaries. Ninety percent of Nagas are now Baptists, though some of their original ceremonies have been transformed and adopted into the new religion.

Since Indian Independence in 1947, Nagaland has become increasingly modernized, and Naga craft work, which has always been greatly admired in the West, has changed character. It is now being produced more commercially as part of a handicraft industry and the highly prized beads, ornaments, carvings, and cloth are sold in markets and bazaars.

Left A spectacular Konyak Naga necklace, with cornelian beads, colored glass beads, bone spacers, and the typical conch shell decorations that were usually set at the nape of the neck and here are also placed on the chest.
Right Rope of glass beads with distinctive button-and-loop-style closure.

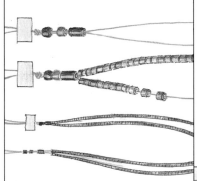

1 Cut 42 strands of 24 inches. Join 2 with an overhand knot 5 inches from one end and tape it down. Thread 1 blue rocaille, 1 orange bead, and 1 red bugle. Separate the strands and thread each with 14 inches of orange beads. Join them and thread on 1 red bugle, 1 orange bead, and 1 blue rocaille, then tie an overhand knot. Thread 20 more double strands.

Naga Necklace

This is a genuine Naga necklace in a typical and time-honored design, probably constructed by a member of the Konyak tribe. It was bought in Delhi from an exiled Tibetan dealer who travels frequently to Nagaland and knows the people well. The necklace is made up of 42 strands, strung in pairs, and has a woven and beaded end section with a button-type fastening. Weaving into the end strands means that the necklace lies flat, but it does not have to be as elaborate or extensive as on the genuine piece. This necklace lies close to the neck, almost like a choker, so you may prefer to lengthen the strands to create a different look.

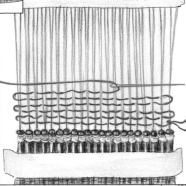

2 Lay the 21 double strands side by side. Starting at the end with the 5-inch threads, comb the strands with your fingers and tape them to the work surface, placing one piece of tape across the last beads and another across the threads about 3½ inches above it. Tie one end of linen thread around the first pair of threads and, using a darning needle, weave it under and over each double strand from one side to the other and back again, pushing each row toward the beads to keep the weaving tight. Continue until you have woven about ½ inch, then finish with a neat and secure knot. Untape.

3 Pair off the threads again and thread on ¾ inch of rocailles and bugles, in the pattern shown (right). Tape down the threads as before and weave another ⅜ inch. Then weave a row of linen thread above and below the red bugles. Make the woven end-piece on the other side of the necklace in the same way.

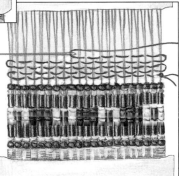

4 (Below) Take 3 pairs of threads from sides and 5 from center of the longer loose ends. Knot and cut off other 10 pairs. Halve middle bunch and overlap ends with the outside bunches, forming 2 loops; tie temporarily with thread. Lay one end of the linen thread ¾ inch along one side of the first bunch and, starting at the base, wind tightly around the loop.

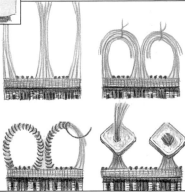

5 (Right) Tie a knot, thread the end through the whipping, and cut off the end. Repeat for the second loop. (Far right, below) On the other side, separate the 5 outer pairs of threads and leave. Knot and tie off the 11 inner pairs. Pull the threads through a fastening coin or button and secure with an overhand knot. Glue before cutting off the ends.

Materials

8 ozs. orange glass beads, ¹⁄₁₆ inch

300 blue, white, and yellow rocailles, ¹⁄₁₆ inch

150 red bugles, ¼ inch

about 33 yards fine polycotton thread

11 yards natural linen thread, for weaving

2 large Indian coins (drilled), buttons or beads

beading needle

darning needle

masking tape

Total length: 19 inches

Lac Beads from Jaipur in Rajasthan

Lac is a resin produced by an insect. It is used to make jewelry such as the colorful bangles and beads worn by the women of Jaipur, as well as the better-known byproducts of varnish and shellac. It is a sticky substance secreted by scale insects to build a nest around their female on the sacred pipal tree. Master craftsman Avaz Mohammed is head of a family of lac beadmakers; the raw resinous material is supplied by his brother, and a second brother sells all the dyes.

Avaz's father, who is 80 years old, melted a basic mixture of shellac, soapstone, and a big brown lump of lac resin over a coal fire. The resulting mix was then used by Avaz, the master. He sat cross-legged before his stove —a rectangle of metal with a small hole, glowing with hot coals.

He took a wooden stick and began to knead the lac, heating it so it would adhere to the stick. One of his daughters, sitting opposite, passed the now-malleable lac constantly over the hot coals to keep it soft—if it hardens, it becomes impossible to work.

The natural brown color of the lac must be dyed; a mixture of kusum and titanium make white, a little red dye added to the white makes pink, while green and blue make black.

The beadmaker then pulled strands of white melted lac off the stick, wound it around his hand like a knitter with a skein of yarn, and set it aside. The soft brown lac was rubbed with black, sticky lac. The white that he had wound around his fingers now looked very much like a bird's nest, but it was adroitly scooped up, crumpled, and integrated with the black, producing wonderfully patterned beads.

They seemed to appear out of nowhere as he twirled and twisted the material, clamped molds over rough shapes before piercing the beads with a long needle to make the holes, and dropping them into water to cool.

Left The Palace of the Winds, the famous symbol of the Pink City of Jaipur, one of the leading centers of lac production.

Above left, from top The master Rajasthani beadmaker demonstrates working the lac resin and winding it into skeins.

Below, from left Lac during the various stages of beadmaking: raw lac resin, the lac ready for working, and examples of lac beads.

Ceramic Beads
from Varanasi

Varanasi on the Ganges is the holiest city in India. At dawn, the pilgrims bathe in the sacred waters and make puja (pray) as the sun rises—a mystical sight. The city is also a renowned bead-making centre, with craftsmen who work with many different materials.

Ram Chandar, a master clay beadmaker, uses clay from a pit near the river. His daughter demonstrates the method here. She picks off lumps of damp clay and rolls them skillfully into perfect globes in seconds, then pierces from each side with a long needle, decorating them with patterns imprinted in the clay.

The beads, produced by the Chandar family and by outworkers, are fired in a traditional kiln, which is fueled first with wood, then with disks of dried cowdung. The beads can be left natural or glazed in traditional designs, simple and attractive, in typical earthy colors by the painters employed by the family.

Tibet: Turquoise, Amber, and dZi

Tibet was, for 500 years, an independent state ruled by a succession of priest-kings, the Dalai Lamas (*lama* means priest). Its Buddhist culture was rich and fascinating, and its bead traditions are of great interest to collectors. In 1959 the Chinese invaded Tibet and the Dalai Lama fled into exile in Dharamsala in northern India, together with many of his people. These refugee Tibetans work in markets and bazaars all over India and Nepal selling traditional artifacts, beads, and jewelry. Some of the other Himalayan groups, such as the mountaineering Sherpas of the Everest region and the Ladakhis of Kashmir, are their cultural cousins. Their Tibetan-style jewelry and beads—wonderful work with silver, turquoise, coral, and bone—can be found in the bazaars of Kathmandu and also in their market towns such as Leh and Namche Bazaar.

Top dZi beads showing the distinctive stripes of banded agate.
Above A Tibetan woman wearing turquoise, amber, coral, and dZi beads.
Left Tibet's Kyi Valley, from the high Kamba La Pass.

Tibetan dZi Beads

Pronounced "d-zee", with the D slurring into the Z, dZi beads are the historic etched agate stone beads from Tibet. Their age is unknown, but they have always been highly prized and are thought to protect the wearer from stroke or lightning. The beads are usually tapered cylinders of dark agate, etched with a geometric pattern consisting of "eyes" (to counteract the Evil Eye) in odd numbers (for good luck) and lines. Currently, the eyes are particularly desirable to bead buyers, especially those from Taiwan, and enormous prices are often paid for perfect specimens with many eyes. As always, beware of glass and plastic imitations.

Turquoise, Amber, and Coral

Turquoise has special significance for Tibetans, but it is prized all over the world. It has been used and admired since before 3000 B.C.: the ancient Egyptians were very fond of its superb color, obtaining supplies of the stone from the Sinai, a source now hardly used except by the Bedouin of Saudi Arabia.

Nowadays the finest turquoise comes from Nishapur in Iran, and it is also mined in the U.S., Russia, Australia, Chile, and China.

Together with amber and coral, turquoise is found in religious jewelry in the entire Himalayan region, including Kashmir, Nepal, and Bhutan. Strings of turquoise and coral are worn through the ears (earrings are considered auspicious). The coral is now sometimes imitation, but the turquoise is almost always real.

Other materials, including glass, can be made to look like turquoise—even Tutankhamun had some glass turquoise in his tomb.

Below An interesting use of favorite Tibetan materials with small beads of turquoise inserted into larger beads of amber, bought in Kathmandu in the 1960s.

Above Two girls from the Himalayan region wearing spectacular hair ornaments of large Burmese amber beads, coral, and turquoise.

Below Typical Tibetan work with large chunks of turquoise and coral tubes.

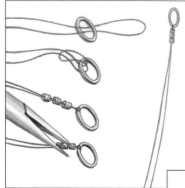

1 Cut twice the length of thread you require, plus an extra 24 inches, and fold it in half. Pass the end loop through a jumpring and feed the loose ends through the loop, pulling them tight to secure the ring to the thread. Attach a beading needle, then thread on 3 crimping beads and squeeze them tightly with pliers to flatten them onto the thread.

2 Thread on a round ⅛-inch silver bead, a decorative silver bead, another round silver bead, and then the turquoise pieces in the planned sequence, interspersing them with round silver beads. When all the turquoise pieces have been used, thread on a round silver bead, a decorative silver bead, and the last round silver bead.

3 Thread on the remaining 3 crimping beads. Pass the thread through the other jumpring, then back through the crimps and the last 3 silver beads.

Necklace of Antique Tibetan Turquoise

This necklace has been assembled from a selection of old Tibetan turquoise pieces separated by silver beads. The seventeen pieces exhibit many different tones of greens and blues, illustrating the variety of colors and range of variegations found in the matrix: traditionally, greener stones are more highly esteemed. Tibetans believe that turquoise and coral offer protection from evil and that, to bring good luck, jewelry should be constructed from an uneven number of stones. This necklace is simple to make and the same method can be used with other stones.

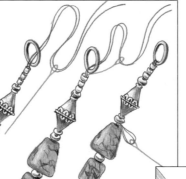

Hints

The turquoise stones should be of varying sizes, so before you begin, lay them out and work out the best threading sequence to complement each shape. Then work out how much doubled thread you will require, allowing for an extra working length of 24 inches.

4 Squeeze the crimps flat with pliers. Knot the loose ends around the main thread, apply a drop of glue, let it dry, then cut off the ends. Use pliers to attach the S-clasp to a jumpring.

Materials

17 assorted turquoise pieces, ½–1¼ inches
20 round silver beads, ⅛ inch
2 decorative silver beads, ⅝ inch
1 silver S-clasp
2 silver jumprings
6 crimping beads
1¾ yards strong linen thread

beading needle
flat-nosed pliers
clear glue
Total length: 17 inches

Lapis Lazuli from Afghanistan

Lapis lazuli, the rich blue stone with golden flecks, has been highly prized since neolithic times. Examples have been found in Egypt from 3000 B.C. and in Central Asia and Pakistan from as early as 6500 B.C.

Lapis is mined in the Badakshan district of Afghanistan, in the mountainous Hindu Kush, near the border with Pakistan. It ranges in color from a deep, rich purple-blue to a greenish blue, often flecked with golden specks of iron pyrites. It contains many minerals, chiefly lazurite, which gives it its blue color. The name comes from the Persian word *lazhward*, meaning the sky, or anything blue.

The remote mines are difficult to reach, and there is a fascinating tale of a 1930s Russian expedition sent to find the source of lapis. The explorers told of a difficult journey at altitude, then suddenly coming upon a glacier covered in white marble rubble containing veins and nests of lapis lazuli in bright blue, pale blue, and darker blue with violet and green tints. Afghanistan, with its red tape, bureaucracy, threats from rebels, Islamic fundamentalists, government troops, and vigilantes, is a dangerous place at any time. But now there is an even greater danger— during the Afghan War of the 1980s, Russian troops, flying helicopters, dropped millions of butterfly mines over the trails and passes in the area. The packhorses and donkeys used to carry the lapis—and their drivers— can unwittingly step on the murderous mines and are blown to pieces.

Even so, the journey to the mine, unique in the world and in all history, is a profitable one. This route winds over icy rivers, snowbound passes, and minefields, all at high altitude. The final half mile is straight up to the entrance of the mine, high up on the mountainside. The entrance leads down a small path into a series of open chambers deep in the mountain where

Above Lapis of AAA grade forms the centerpiece for this necklace recently made in Peshawar. The small lapis beads are interspersed with gold beads in the style of ancient Egyptian collars.

Below Strands of deep blue lapis: the classic round beads are regarded as showing off the color to best advantage. The very thin strand consists of minute beads, a tribute to the enormous skill of the Afghan beadmaker.

Above A lapis beadmaker in Afghanistan. The stone is mined in the mountains, and carried down on donkey-back to the market at Peshawar in Pakistan.

Right The Blue Mosque at Mazaq-i-Sherif, one of the most important religious sites in Afghanistan. Blue is an important color in the Islamic faith, and splendid blue-tiled mosques are seen all over Central Asia.

Above A necklace of
Afghan lapis lazuli disks
and Indian-made silver
beads and clasp.
Right Distinctive necklaces
of lapis, silver, and cornelian.
Afghan silverwork is of high
quality and shows its
cultural links with the
Islamic world of the Middle
East and North Africa, and
with other cultures of the
Indian subcontinent.

the miners chisel and hammer away at the cave walls. From this seam came every piece, every inch, every tiny morsel of lapis throughout history. Dynamite is used to loosen the rock, followed by a more low-tech chiseling and hammering. Finally the lumps of stone, glowing pure and perfect blue, are put into sacks to be carried down the precipitous slope to the horses and donkeys waiting far below. The porters slide the sacks down the icy slopes to set off any stray mines before venturing down themselves.

Buying and selling takes place in the city of Peshawar in Pakistan but only in the morning when the sun best shows the intensity of color. The dealers meet in a large room in complete silence. Under the long sleeves of the traditional *salwar kameez*, a purchaser grasps the dealer's fingers and, in a complicated series of signals, establishes a price without anyone else in the room knowing the result.

The seam is the finest in the world. It runs north into Russia, where some lapis is also found, and there is a very inferior deposit in Chile. The danger is that after thousands of years, there is only about 30 years' worth of lapis left in Afghanistan if it continues to be extracted at the current rate.

Counterfeit Lapis Lazuli

Ancient Egyptians made artificial (or reconstituted) lapis of powdered lapis formed into a paste. It was used for making beads, while the real thing was reserved for scarabs and the figures of gods. Today lapis is still faked: either made synthetically, or by dying poor-quality lapis a richer color (though a dab of nail polish remover will soon reveal that to a purchaser).

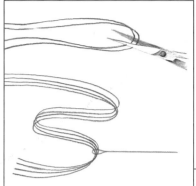

1 Lay out the lapis lazuli disks and beads, placing the largest in the center and graduating to the smallest at both ends. Cut the silk thread into 4 equal lengths to form a 4-ply strand on which to thread the beads. Thread a beading needle onto one end of the strand.

2 Thread on the ¾-inch lapis disk and leave it in the center of the strand. Add 1 silver disk spacer, 3 lapis cylinders, 1 spacer, 1 large round, 1 spacer, 3 cylinders, 1 spacer, a ⅝-inch disk, 1 spacer, 3 cylinders, 1 spacer, 1 medium round, 1 spacer, 3 cylinders, 1 spacer, a ⅝-inch disk, 1 spacer, 3 cylinders, 1 spacer, 1 medium round, 1 spacer, 3 cylinders, 1 spacer, a ½-inch disk, 1 spacer, 3 cylinders, 1 spacer, 1 small round, 1 spacer, and 4 cylinders. Make a temporary knot at the end.

3 Thread the needle onto the 4 strands on the other side of the necklace and add the small lapis lazuli cylinder that will act as the end stopper. Thread the needle back up through the ¾-inch disk and the first silver spacer. Then thread the other side of the necklace, following the bead sequence in reverse.

Necklace of Lapis Lazuli Discs

This necklaces is made from small lapis cylinders, larger flat disks (pierced through their sides rather than in the center of the disk) and a few round beads that are interspersed with tiny silver beads to highlight the different shades of blue. This lapis is not the deepest of blues, but it has attractive markings produced by the matrix, or surrounding stone, in which the lapis formed. The construction of the necklace is simple, but the holes in the beads must be large enough to take a number of silk strands, which will then be twisted to form an attractive rope.

Hint
If you wish, vary the design by adding a contrasting stone such as cornelian. You can also alter the length of the rope or wear 2 strings together.

4 Unthread the needle and tie an overhand knot as close to the last cylinder as possible. Divide the 4 threads into pairs and twist each pair separately. Taking care not to release the tension, knot the ends together and the twisted pairs will wind together to form a cord. Repeat on the other side of the necklace and join the 2 sides with an overhand knot.

Materials

7 flat lapis lazuli disks, 1 of
  ¾ inch diameter, 4 of
  ⅝ inch, 2 of ½ inch
8 round lapis lazuli beads,
  2 of ³⁄₁₆ inch, 4 of ¼ inch,
  2 of ⅛ inch
1 lapis lazuli cylinder, ¹⁄₁₆ inch

50 lapis lazuli cylinders,
  ⅛ inch
29 silver disks, ¹⁄₃₂ inch
5 yards blue silk thread
beading needle
Total length: 32 inches

The East
and Oceania

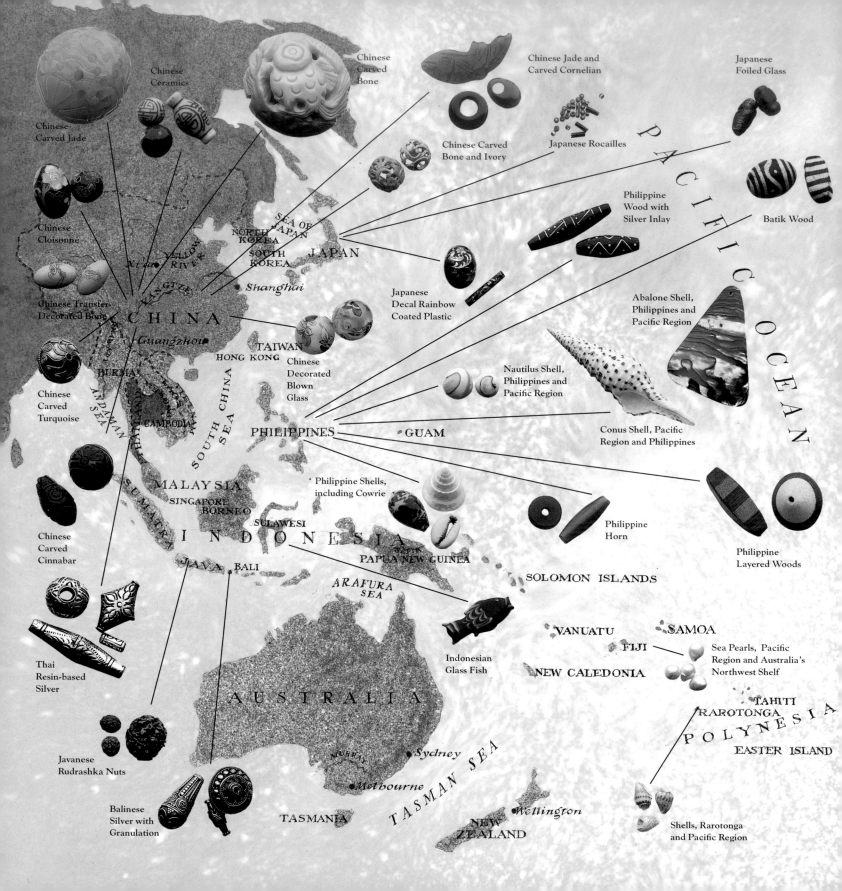

Chinese Ceramics

Chinese Carved Bone

Chinese Jade and Carved Cornelian

Japanese Foiled Glass

Chinese Carved Jade

Chinese Carved Bone and Ivory

Japanese Rocailles

Chinese Cloisonne

Philippine Wood with Silver Inlay

Batik Wood

PACIFIC OCEAN

Chinese Transfer-Decorated Bone

Abalone Shell, Philippines and Pacific Region

Japanese Decal Rainbow Coated Plastic

Chinese Carved Turquoise

Chinese Decorated Blown Glass

Nautilus Shell, Philippines and Pacific Region

Conus Shell, Pacific Region and Philippines

Chinese Carved Cinnabar

Philippine Shells, including Cowrie

Philippine Horn

Philippine Layered Woods

Thai Resin-based Silver

Indonesian Glass Fish

Sea Pearls, Pacific Region and Australia's Northwest Shelf

Javanese Rudrashka Nuts

Balinese Silver with Granulation

Shells, Rarotonga and Pacific Region

SEA OF JAPAN
NORTH KOREA
SOUTH KOREA
JAPAN
Xi'an
YELLOW RIVER
Shanghai
YANGTZE
CHINA
Guangzhou
TAIWAN
HONG KONG
BURMA
ANDAMAN SEA
THAILAND
MEKONG
CAMBODIA
SOUTH CHINA SEA
PHILIPPINES
GUAM
MALAYSIA
SINGAPORE
BORNEO
SUMATRA
INDONESIA
SULAWESI
JAVA
BALI
PAPUA NEW GUINEA
ARAFURA SEA
SOLOMON ISLANDS
VANUATU
SAMOA
FIJI
NEW CALEDONIA
AUSTRALIA
TAHITI
RAROTONGA
POLYNESIA
EASTER ISLAND
MURRAY
Sydney
Melbourne
TASMAN SEA
TASMANIA
NEW ZEALAND
Wellington

This vast area, from northern Asia to Polynesia, including China, Japan, Southeast Asia, Australia and New Zealand, boasts diverse cultures, and some of the greatest of ancient civilizations.

It has been said that Marco Polo's thirteenth-century tales of the East may not have been the result of his own first-hand experience, but they are still romantic. He spoke of pearl fishing and ruby mines, lapis lazuli and coral, prayer beads as worn by mighty kings, cowrie currency, spices, silks, silver mines, and gold dust. Until then, little of the many diverse cultures, climates, histories, and traditions of the Far East were known to the people of medieval and Renaissance Europe.

In China (ancient Cathay) beads have been found in imperial tombs, yet except for the ruling classes and the wealthy, the wearing of jewelry was not universally popular in China.

Previous pages This collection of necklaces from the Far East includes: black coral necklace from the Philippines; shell belt from Papua New Guinea; a string of hand-decorated Chinese porcelain beads; shell necklace from Luzon, the Philippines; Balinese granulated silver beads.

Top right A seed belt strung with grass from Papua New Guinea.
Above Japanese netsuke, made from a tagua nut, of a monk holding a plum for longevity. Netsukes were also made from ivory, wood, lacquer, horn and bamboo.
Left Miao women from southern China, wearing spectacular silver beads.
Right Painted ivory beads from the 1950s, before the use of ivory was prohibited.

Today, it is the world's largest producer of semiprecious beads, made from imported stones. Cloisonné, handpainted porcelain, and blown glass beads are also widely produced.

Tiny objects commanding extremely high prices among collectors are the Japanese netsukes and ojimes, worn on the kimono. These restrained subtle miniature antique works of art can are often be breathtakingly complex, depicting subjects from history and literature.

Japanese art has always been renowned for its purity, and modern Japan now has a large bead industry that specializes particularly in beautiful rocailles, glass, plastic, and imitation pearls.

Silverwork has long been a Southeast Asian tradition, especially in Vietnam, Bali, and Thailand. First brought to the area by Indian traders 2,000 years ago, many designs are derived from Hindu and Buddhist images, often reflected in modern beads from these parts.

Chinese Jade

Jade has been treasured by the Chinese for more than 7,000 years. They called it *yu*, and it was used in burials to preserve the corpse intact, in religious and rainmaking ceremonies, and is generally considered to be the "good luck stone."

Jade varies in color from a milky translucence to the finest emerald green imperial jade. In 1863 it was discovered that jade comes in two forms, nephrite and jadeite, both gemstones with similar properties. Most prized in China was jadeite, the imperial jade, which comes from Myanmar (Burma). There is a story of a thirteenth-century Chinese trader in Burma who picked up a piece of stone to balance the load on his mule. When he returned home, he discovered that the "stone" was a piece of the finest jade. He hurried back to Burma to locate the source but never found it. It was not until hostilities ceased between China and Burma in the eighteenth century that this jade was mined commercially.

The Chinese and Japanes treasure jade. In ancient times, working it was very difficult. It is extremely hard, and carving intricate pieces was a lengthy process, sometimes using only water, a hollow bamboo rod, and abrasive sand. It was first sawn into blocks and then ground or drilled using sharp stones or metal. Abrasive quartz sand or diamond particles were used to grind the carvings, which could then be polished with wood, leather, or stone. Modern methods are much less time-consuming.

Fake Jade

Many green stones are given exotic names and passed off as jade: Indian (green aventurine quartz), Manchurian (soapstone), Korean (bowenite serpentine), Transvaal (massive grossularite garnet), Amazon (green microcline feldspar), Styrian (pseudophite), and Soo Chow jade. All are green stones, but often dyed to enhance their color. Connemara marble, bowenite and even jadeolite are frequently described as "jade". Be aware also that B-quality jade is jadeite with its brown staining removed by acid and the color enhanced.

Many of these stones are beautiful in their own right, as long as you are not paying a jade price for an inferior material. A good exercise is to seek out a necklace of authentic jade, feel it, and study it, and note its price, before buying a cheaper simulated stone. Then, if you like the stone, that is all that's important.

Above Antique Chinese jade pendant with knotting and tassel work. The perforations in this piece were painstakingly carved by hand in a very time-consuming process, jade being one of the hardest of all semiprecious stones.
Right The Chinese used personal seals much as they were used in the West. These have been knotted together with carved animal zodiac figures.

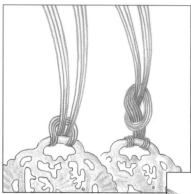

1 Fold the 4 strands of thread in half and pass the end loop through the top of the pendant. Pass the loose ends through the loop to hang the pendant on the center of the strands. Tie an overhand knot as close as possible to the pendant.

Jade Pendant

This onyx necklace has a beautifully carved Chinese jade pendant as its centerpiece. Similar pieces can be found in the Chinatown areas of big cities and in the Far East. The fine green and black onyx beads that make up the necklace are widely available. Onyx is part of the agate family and can be identified by its milky white bands interspersed with brown. The black onyx beads are formed by immersing them first in a hot sugar solution, then in concentrated sulfuric acid, and then finally applying heat. Each bead is individually knotted onto the strand for safety and to prevent it from rubbing against the others; it is important to tie neat, uniform knots.

2 Divide the 8 strands into 2 pairs and thread a black onyx bead onto one 4-ply side. Form a loose overhand knot in the thread next to the bead. Holding the loose ends in one hand, insert the tweezers or pliers into the loop and grasp the thread right next to the bead.

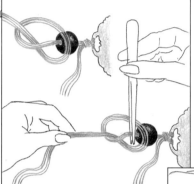

3 Gently pull the long thread to tighten the knot onto the tweezers, making sure the 4 threads tighten at the same rate. Add beads in the following order, forming a knot after each in the same way: 4 black beads, 1 green bead, 4 black, 1 green, 4 black, 1 green, and 18 black. Repeat the process to form the other side of the necklace.

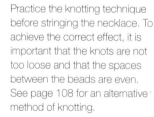

Hint

Practice the knotting technique before stringing the necklace. To achieve the correct effect, it is important that the knots are not too loose and that the spaces between the beads are even. See page 108 for an alternative method of knotting.

Materials

carved jade pendant,
    2 x 2½ inches

62 black onyx beads, ¼ inch

6 green onyx beads, ⅜ inch

5 yards green silk thread,
    cut into 4 equal lengths

1 inch gimp, cut in half

2 jumprings

1 S-clasp

beading needle

tweezers or small needle–
    nosed pliers

clear glue

Total length excluding
    pendant: 30 inches

4 Thread a piece of gimp and a jumpring onto each side. Pass the needle back through the last bead, easing the gimp into a neat loop to protect the thread. Divide the strands into 2 pairs and knot them around the main thread. Apply a drop of glue to the knot and let it dry before cutting off the ends. Using pliers, attach the S-clasp to a jumpring.

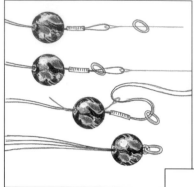

1 Double the silk and thread on the needle. Thread on a bead, a piece of gimp, and the ring side of the clasp. Slide the bead, gimp, and ring to the center of the thread, then pass the needle back through the bead and ease the gimp into a small loop around the ring to protect the thread.

Cloisonné Necklace

Cloisonné is an ancient artform in China. Metal wires are applied to a metal base, then enamels are dropped into the spaces. The piece is then fired so the enamel melts into the shape edged by the wires. This is repeated several times.

Since the beads are ornate, they are best strung simply. The knotting between each bead means they sit slightly away from each other, emphasizing their shape and decoration. The knots should be large enough to prevent them being engulfed by the holes. The knotting requires a good deal of practice, but this method is probably the simplest for a beginner. It can be used for restringing pearls or other precious beads.

2 Loosely form an overhand knot next to the bead by wrapping the 4 strands of thread around your index finger, then threading the loose ends through the loop formed.

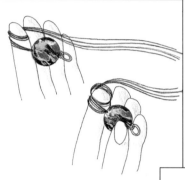

3 Insert a thick needle into the loop before tightening it. As you tighten the knot onto the needle, pull it up against the bead, then remove the needle and pull tight, making sure the 4 strands tighten at the same rate to form a perfect knot right next to the bead. Continue this knotting process until you have used up all the beads.

Hint

To calculate the thread required, measure the length of your beads and multiply by the number you are using. Multiply this amount by 4 if you wish to use 4-ply thread, then double your total for the knotting. Allow an extra working length of 12 inches. Page 106 gives an alternative method.

Materials

25 round cloisonné beads,
   ½ inch

4 yards silk thread

½ inch gimp, cut in half

1 gold clip clasp and ring

beading needle

tapestry needle

clear glue

Total length: 18 inches

4 Thread on the other piece of gimp and the clip side of the clasp. Pass the needle back through the last bead, pulling the thread taut and easing the gimp around the loop on the clasp. Divide the threads into 2 pairs and knot them around the main thread. Apply a drop of glue to the knot and let it dry before cutting off the ends.

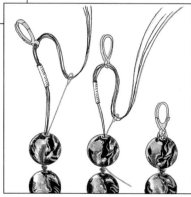

Sea Pearls and Freshwater Pearls

From earliest times, the natural pearl was among the most prized of all jewels. Found inside oyster shells, pearls have been fished by divers off the coasts of Sri Lanka and Australia, in the Persian Gulf and the Red Sea, and in the South Seas off the Tuamoto archipelago. The divers risked their lives as they plunged 50 to 100 feet on one lungful of air, searching for oysters, swiftly prizing them off the rocks with hands or knives, putting them in a sack, then quickly returning to the surface for air. The life of the pearl diver was never an easy one.

The pearl has always been surrounded by myth and legend, giving it a mystical quality unsurpassed by any other gem. It was considered by many cultures to be the supernatural product of fire and water, or of divine origin. The Chinese believed the rain god, in the form of the sky dragon, released droplets into the sea during storms that settled in oyster and mussel shells, and the Romans believed oysters opened in the season for procreation and were impregnated by dew.

Many of the pearls from Roman and Renaissance times came from the Persian Gulf. There

Right Cultured pearls are grown in various places around the world. This is Naga Noi Pearl Farm on a small island off Phuket in Thailand. This farm worker is sorting open oyster shells where blister pearls have been formed on the inside shells. The pearls will be cut off the shell, then used in items of jewelry such as flat earrings and brooches, from which only one side of the pearl will be seen. Fine round pearls are formed by putting the spherical bead inside the oyster rather than attaching it to the shell.

Below left Strands of cultured freshwater pearls showing the variety of colors that are being produced through modern methods of laser dyeing.

were also sources in Europe and in North America—freshwater pearls have been found many Scottish rivers, such as the Tay and the Doon, for more than 2,000 years. The River Conwy in Wales and streams in Ireland, France, Austria, and Germany have also been fished for pearls. River pearls are also found in Nova Scotia and in streams in the Mississippi valley.

Cultured Pearls

Many experiments were made to stimulate the oysters to produce pearls, but none was commercially viable until a Japanese noodle seller named Mikimoto became interested in pearls and patented a process in 1896 to produce what became known as cultured pearls. A spherical mother-of-pearl bead was introduced between the shells of the pearl oyster and the irritant was soon covered by nacre. Later, after World War I, the technique was perfected, and European markets first saw cultured pearls produced by this method in 1921. Most cultured pearl farmers today use a mother-of-pearl spherical bead cut from the Mississippi pig-toe mussel as the basis of their pearls.

Pollution has now stopped production of one of the most famous cultured pearls, the

Biwa freshwater pearl cultivated in Biwa-ko (*ko* means "lake"), in Japan. Freshwater mussels were grafted with tissue from another mussel in up to 20 places and, after much experimentation, produced small rice-shaped pearls. If the extraction was done carefully, a second and third crop from the same mussel was possible without further grafting.

The first crop of pearls was harvested in 1925, but nowadays Biwa-ko is too polluted to produce these pearls. The Chinese have initiated a pearl industry producing lower-quality pearls, or "rice krispies" as they are also known, which are available at low prices. The quality of production has much improved, and it is now possible to obtain a semi-round freshwater pearl that is very attractive.

Because these freshwater pearls do not have a nucleus or small bead inside, the nacre is much thicker than even in some cultured pearls. When buying, make sure you choose strings of regularly shaped pearls with a fine color and lustrous sheen, and avoid any with chalky white coloring and odd shapes.

Left These large cultured pearls have a wonderful lustrous colour and are very well-matched. Pearls of this size are becoming scarce and therefore expensive. It is said that pearls are a fine investment and will increase in value, unlike diamonds.

Above Glass pearls have been coated with a nacre-like substance to make them resemble real pearls.

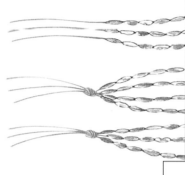

10 strands of thread together at one end with a loose overhand knot and tape it down. Thread a fine-wire needle onto 1 strand and thread on the pearls. Repeat with the remaining 9 strands, making sure that you make each strand approximately the same length. Tie a secure knot at the end of each strand as you complete it.

1 For 32-inch strands: smooth out the strands on the work surface, gather them together at one end, tie a loose overhand knot, and tape it down. Unknot the other ends of each strand and remove some beads so the strands are the desired length. For 16-inch strands: carefully unthread all the pearls and collect them in a container. Tie the

2 (Above) Carefully undo the temporary knot and secure each end with a knot close to the last bead. Divide the strands into two bundles of 3 strands and one of 4. Knot each bundle together as close as possible to the last beads on both ends.

3 To attach the bundles to the clasp, take one end of a group of 3 strands and thread it through one of the outer holes in the clasp, fastening it with a secure knot. Do not cut off the ends. Using the same method, attach the group of 4 strands to the center hole in the clasp, and the remaining group of 3 strands to the other outer hole. Attach the other end of each strand to the corresponding hole on the other part of the clasp.

Materials

18 strands of freshwater
   pearls (16-inch
   strands) or 10
   strands of 32-inch
12 yards silk thread, cut
   into 10 equal lengths
3-strand clasp
fine-wire needle (see
   Hint)
clear glue
masking tape
Total length: 28 inches

Ten-strand Necklace of Freshwater Pearls

Freshwater pearls are now widely available, and the only difficulty might be in obtaining pearls of the right quality. If you are lucky, you will find pearls with a beautiful luster, that will be shown to best advantage *en masse*. This necklace is not at all difficult to make; if you want to create a necklace of the same length, it will be even easier if you can find pearls strung in 32-inch strands, although they are generally sold in 16-inch strands. If you are lucky enough to find double-length strands you won't even need to rethread the pearls. Choose strands that match in size and color.

Hint
To string beads with very small holes, make a needle of the finest gauge wire: cut a 4-inch length of wire, bend it in half, and twist it together, leaving the folded end in a large loop to form an eye for the thread.

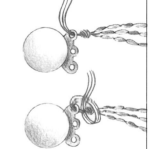

4 When you are sure that you have attached the clasp correctly, secure each knot with a drop of glue and let it dry before cutting off the ends.

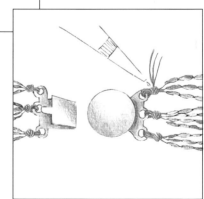

113

Japanese Glass

Japan is now a major force in the production of seed beads (or rocailles) and bugles. Their glass factories produce high-quality, uniform beads in myriad colors and finishes unequaled anywhere else in the world.

Rocailles are the tiny beads that constitute much of the beadwork jewelry that has been made by indigenous peoples all over the world. Called margarite beads since the sixteenth century by European traders, they have also been known as pound beads (sold by the pound), seed beads (not to be confused with natural seeds), and rocailles (little rocks). They are made in a variety of sizes from ½ to ¼ inch and larger. Bugles are tube beads made in the same way.

There are eight basic steps required to make rocaille beads from the drawn glass canes, and each step is completed by a different team of workers. First, the raw material is created by heating the constituents of the glass (silica sand, soda ash, plus various other chemicals to produce the colors), in varying quantities in a large furnace at over 2370°F and for at least 18 hours until the mixture becomes molten.

Right A contemporary multistrand graduated necklace using fine and delicate glass rocailles (seed) beads interspersed with larger beads used as a contrast.

Above This Japanese girl in traditional dress wears a fine beaded hairpiece.

Left These glass "delicas" beads are a relatively new development, unique to the Japanese. An amazing variety of finishes and colors is available, making them suitable for embroidery and fine beadwork, in the same way that rocailles provided the raw materials for cultures as diverse as the Masai in Africa, the Naga people in India, and Native Americans.

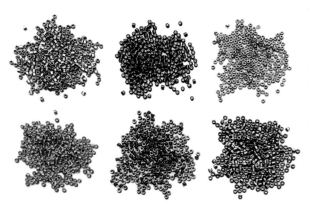

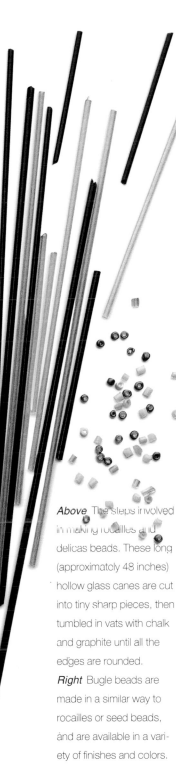

Far left The process of making rocailles showing the long canes with small holes running their length, ready for cutting

Left The raw materials for making glass are mixed together in this factory.

The glass is is "drawn", or pulled, out of the furnace down a metal channel 50 yards long, and gradually turns from molten red to the color of the finished glass. The hole is formed by passing air through a blowpipe in the molten glass in the holding furnace, and the speed of pulling determines the diameter of the hole. This cane is cut into three-foot lengths, which are calibrated into sizes by specialist machinery that judges the diameter of the cane.

Bundles of canes are laid lengthwise in a machine that chops the glass cane into small chips. They fly out of the machine like fine powder and are caught in a large tub.

Each tiny chip is now the basis of a bead, but is extremely sharp. A fine powder of wood carbon, chalk, graphite, and salt is mixed with the glass chippings and reheated to 1450–1650°F for approximately 30 to 45 minutes to round the edges of the beads.

The graphite is washed off in hydrofluoric acid and water, and the beads are dried in centrifugal machines. The powder mixture can be shaken off the beads to be recycled. Various finishes may now added to the beads. Silver lining is achieved by washing in water and a chemical to remove silvering from the outside of a bead, color dyes can be added, fire polishing entails reheating in an oven with chemicals that will adhere to the glass, and rainbow finish gives an iridescent effect.

The beads are re-sorted and packed into the correct sizes. A simple but effective machine tests each bead individually to guarantee it has a hole and that it is the correct size. They are packed into one-pound plastic bags.

Above The steps involved in making rocailles and delicas beads. These long (approximately 48 inches) hollow glass canes are cut into tiny sharp pieces, then tumbled in vats with chalk and graphite until all the edges are rounded.

Right Bugle beads are made in a similar way to rocailles or seed beads, and are available in a variety of finishes and colors.

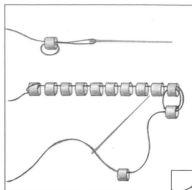

1 Once you have planned a design, start on the main body of the bracelet. Thread the needle onto a manageable length of thread. Leaving a loose end of about 6 inches to make the end section (see step 4), thread twice through the first bead to secure it, then thread on the first row of 10 beads.

Delicas Bracelet

Delicas are modern cylinder rocaille (or seed) beads developed in Japan. Traditional rocailles are formed from long tubes or rods of glass, which are cut into tiny pieces and then tumbled to achieve a round shape. They have a tendency to be slightly uneven, especially in the larger sizes, which is particularly noticeable when they are used in a weaving process. Delicas have perfect, uniform roundness, allowing them to be woven into a smooth design. A square flat stitch has been used so the beads lie in rows. Once you have mastered the technique of weaving with a needle and without a loom, you will be able to create your own designs, perhaps for a small bag.

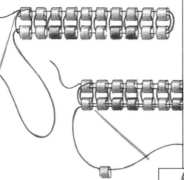

2 To start the second row, place the eleventh bead along-side the tenth bead. Pass the thread through the eleventh, back through the tenth, and out through the eleventh. To proceed, thread through the bead in the second row, around the corresponding bead in the previous row and back through the bead you are joining.

3 For added strength, once you have completed a row, run the needle through the beads on the previous row and return it through the row of beads you have just finished. Continue building up the design using the same stitch.

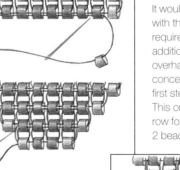

Materials

¾ oz. cylinder rocailles,
  ⅟₁₆ inch, in 12 colors
4½ yards beading thread
1 figure-eight clasp and
  hook
size 12 beading needle
Dimensions: ⅝ x 7½ inches

4 For the end sections, bring the needle out of the penulti-mate bead in the last row; this is where the row of 8 beads will start. Continue the stitching, leaving off one bead on each outside edge for the next 3 rows, then make 2 rows with just 2 beads. Sew the clasp onto one end and the hook onto the other. Finish with firm knots.

Hint

It would be impossible to work with the length of thread required in a single piece; attach additional lengths with a double overhand knot, which can be concealed inside a bead. The first step is to finalize the design. This one contains 10 beads per row for 82 rows, decreasing by 2 beads a row at each end.

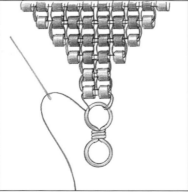

Balinese Silver Beadwork

The techniques of silver beadmaking are very similar all over the world, but each community has developed and refined its own style. Bali in particular, and Southeast Asia as a whole, have strong silversmithing traditions, that were introduced, it is believed, by traders from India. The Indians brought their religions with them, and both Buddhism and Hinduism spread across Southeast Asia. Later, Islam gained converts too, and today much of Malaysia and most of Indonesia is

Above A representative example of Balinese bead designs, showing the wide variety of styles produced using fine granulation and wire work.

Left Terraced fields of rice paddy on Bali. This tiny Indonesian island is the last vestige of Hindu culture in a country that is now predominantly Muslim.

Above right Bali is a largely agricultural society. This farmer is ploughing his paddy fields with cattle. The cow is a holy animal in the Hindu religion, but their sacred status does not prevent them from working.

Muslim. Only Bali remained resolutely and picturesquely Hindu, with its own versions of traditional Hindu arts and crafts, such as dance and jewelry-making.

Silverworking in Southeast Asia makes great use of hammering, embossing (repoussé), engraving, and openwork, inlay, filigree, and granulation, and it is granulation in particular that is the hallmark of modern Balinese silver beads. The tradition of this work is very old, but during the past few decades, a new and thriving industry has developed.

The Balinese use the same techniques found in India, Nepal, Vietnam, Morocco, Ethiopia, Mexico, and South America. Silver can be obtained from melting down silver coins, but in Bali is bought in small pellets that are melted and then mixed with copper to strengthen the alloy. This liquid mix is poured into molds and then, when hardened, it is repeatedly squeezed

Right Silver wire and granulations being applied to a half-cup silver bead. The two halves of the bead are decorated separately, lying flat on their equators, then soldered together.

between rollers to form a thin, flat sheet, which is then hammered to form half-cup shapes. When the halves are complete, they are soldered together before being decorated.

The beads are decorated with silver wires and granulation balls. The wires are made with a metal template perforated with different-sized holes. A fat piece of silver is pulled through progressively smaller and smaller holes to form a silver wire. The tiny granulation balls are made in quantity. The wire is wound around the bead to form shapes—hearts, triangles, zigzags, and whorls—which are then filled with granulations. Alternatively, tiny holes are made to produce openwork designs.

The completed bead is cleaned, polished, and sometimes given a black "antiquing" or oxidizing coating to make it look old.

Left Balinese necklace, showing beads decorated with appliquéd wire and silver granulation balls.

Above Balinese silver factory, with the bead-makers sitting at benches on the veranda.

Balinese Earrings and Necklace

These elegant earrings and necklace contain superb examples of Balinese silverwork at its finest. The beads are set out in pairs, separated by tiny granulated disks.

The earrings can be lengthened by adding extra small beads; do not add any more large beads or the earrings will become too heavy to wear. You might prefer to make the necklace shorter or simpler, depending on how many silver beads you can track down—not necessarily from Bali.

Materials

2 round beads, ¾ inch	2 tiny faceted beads,
2 round beads, ⅜ inch	¹⁄₁₆ inch
2 small granulated disks,	2 silver headpins, 2 inches
¼ inch	2 silver ear-hooks
4 tiny granulated disks,	wire cutters
⅛ inch	round-nosed pliers

1 Thread the beads onto the headpin in the following sequence: 1 tiny faceted bead, 1 round ¾-inch bead, 1 tiny granulated disk, 1 round ⅜-inch bead, another tiny granulated disk, and finally 1 small granulated disk.

2 Using pliers, grasp the headpin just above the last bead and bend it to form a right angle. Cut off the extra length, leaving about ¼ inch.

3 Grasp the wire with pliers and roll them over to form a loop, but before closing it, pass it through the loop on the ear-hook. Squeeze the loop shut, making sure the wire end touches the stem above the last bead, so it forms a perfect loop. To make the second earring, repeat the steps as above.

1 Lay out the beads with the largest in the center and graduating to the smallest at both ends. Fold the thread in half and pass the folded end through one of the jumprings. Feed the cut ends through the loop and pull them tight to secure the jumpring to the thread. Thread the needle onto the cut ends.

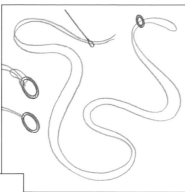

2 Beginning with 2 tiny plain silver disks, thread on the beads in the planned sequence, interspersing each with a granulated disk and finishing with 2 tiny silver disks.

3 Pass the thread through the other jumpring and secure it with a tight double knot as close to the last bead as possible. Thread the ends back through the last 3 beads and knot them around the main thread. Apply a drop of glue to the knot and let it dry before cutting off the ends. Use pliers to attach the S-clasp to a jumpring.

Materials

approximately 100 silver beads, graduating from ⅛–¾ inch

80 tiny granulated disks, ¼ inch

4 tiny plain silver disks, ⅛ inch

2 yards linen or spun nylon thread

2 silver jumprings

1 silver S-clasp

beading needle

clear glue

Total length: 35 inches

Thai Silver

Thai silver beads are a relatively recent arrival onto the world bead scene, but they have become very popular. Ban Kwao is a village specializing in silverwork, and there is a constant noise of tap-tap-tap-tapping that echoes around the village. Everywhere you turn there is another workshop with the artisans hard at work on their silver beads.

Workshops are set up on the shady verandas of wooden houses set on stilts. Each bead takes 20 to 30 minutes to make, and each person, working a 10-hour day, carries out one process, handing the bead onto the next person in the production line.

Two thousand beads are produced each month in this village alone, so if you wear a necklace of 40 Thai silver beads you are wearing the equivalent of two days' output of a village like this.

The raw silver is bought in little balls. These are heated until they form a lump, which is

Right Silver is rolled into long, thin strips on a hand-operated machine.
Below A Hmong woman wearing the distinctive large silver beads of her tribe.
Below left Many Thai men spend a period of their lives as Buddhist monks.

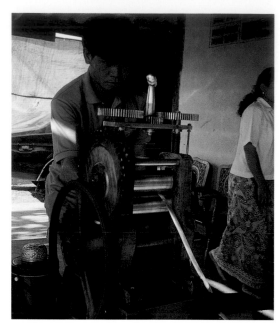

Below The stages of Thai beadmaking; thin silver sheets are wound around a bamboo cane to form a tube, top and bottom are soldered, then filled with a mixture of pig oil, rubber, and soya before being decorated.

then rolled into a long, thin, silver strip on a machine that is wound by hand. That strip is then run around a bamboo cane to form a tube, and the join is sealed with solder.

A short metal rod, with protruding pieces like sawn-off branches of a tree, is used as the rim-former. The edge of the hollow tube is placed against one of the protuberances and a rim or lip is tapped out with a small hammer. A metal wire ring made of copper and silver is then soldered onto both rims.

The hollow shape is rinsed with a mixture of lime, salt, and water to whiten the blackened silver, and the shapes are stuffed with a mixture

of soya, plantation rubber, and pig oil, which looks rather like lac, and is soft and malleable. The bead is now solid, but still without a hole.

The patterns are applied with a variety of household objects, including razors and ball-point pens, then a hole is made using a piece of hot wire. The beads are cleaned with detergent and a wire brush. To achieve an "antique effect" they leave the beads to soak in black hair dye for four hours.

Traditional Silverwork

Modern Thai silver has found immediate acceptance in the markets of Europe, the Far East, and America. However, traditional silverwork worn by the tribes of the Golden Triangle of Thailand, Burma, and Laos has always been of great interest to anthropologists as well as bead collectors.

The Akha, Karen, Hmong (also known as the Miao), Lahu, and Lisu wear beautiful silverwork, and the Akha and Hmong are especially known for the huge silver beads forming part of their traditional headdresses. Other materials are also used, including brass and copper, Chinese glass trade beads, and shells. The massive, finely made silver beads worn by young women form their dowry and, traditionally, spare money was converted into dowry beads.

Above A necklace bought in Chang Mai, Northern Thailand, with lotus-bud beads made in the usual silverworking manner, but using metal from brass shell cases, leftover from the wars in Southeast Asia.

Below, from left This beadmaker showing the processes described on the previous page.

The Philippines

The Philippines were annexed by Spain in 1571, ceded to the United States in 1898, and gained independence in 1946. Though many of the people now wear westernized dress, there are a number of ethnic groups who still wear traditional clothing and beads, especially for ceremonial occasions.

Beadmaking as an industry began only in the 1970s with the new vogue for beaded jewelry. Working with materials found locally such as wood, shell, seeds, and clay, the Philippines is now a world force in craft production.

Wooden Beads

Local woods, such as palmwood, are always used. Beads are made from cubes cut out of strips of wood in which the holes have been drilled first. A simple tool, a stick with about an inch of wire protruding, is inserted into the hole so the bead can be held against a grinding wheel to form the shape. Sometimes the rough cubes are strung onto a length of wire attached to a bowlike apparatus and the craftsman holds them against the grinding wheel to achieve uniformly rounded shapes. When shaped, the beads are tumbled in a drum with wax to add shine, or dyed or spray-painted before being threaded into 16-inch strings.

Painted Beads

Large beads are handpainted with wonderful imagination. First, a stick is inserted into the "blank" or raw wooden bead, which is painted and allowed to dry before being decorated with the design. A finished batch of beads still on their sticks looks like a mass of lollipops. They are then taken off the sticks and packed for shipment around the world.

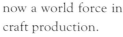

Above Young men wearing shell beads at the Masskara Parade, Bacalod on Negros Island.
Right Disks are stamped out of the raw shell, in preparation for beadmaking.

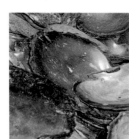  

Stonecutting

Local stones are preferred, but semiprecious stones are also used. The methods used for stonecutting are very like those used for wooden beads, except that water must be sprayed constantly onto the stone to prevent it from overheating. The stone is cut into strips, then cubes, and then drilled. The stick-tool is then inserted and the beads are held against the grinding wheel to form the correct shape.

Shell Beads and Coco Beads

Some shell beads are made with a "marquetry" process. A beautiful effect is obtained by laying different pieces of shell onto a wooden base, covering them in epoxy resin, then, when dry, grinding off the resin to reveal the shell underneath. The same method can be used with wood.

Other beads (and buttons) are made from trochus shells and the black and brown lip shell. Coco beads are made in the same way. After sorting and cleaning, the shells are punched under a drill with a circular cutting tool, and the blanks, with holes already drilled, are threaded onto strings and ground smooth. In the case of coco beads, they are then bleached in hydrogen peroxide before being dyed and put into tumbling machines with clear white furniture wax to make them smooth and shiny.

Opposite, above Strips are cut from mother-of-pearl, applied to wooden bases, covered with epoxy resin, scraped back, and polished.
Center left Necklaces of nautilus shell beads, pearls, 1920s mother-of-pearl square beads, and old shell disks.
Left From top: wooden beads are cut into strips, then drilled, rounded, carved, and polished.

125

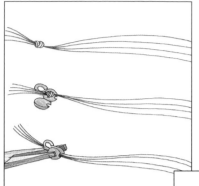

1 Cut the thread into 4 equal lengths, gather them together, and join them with a double overhand knot in one end. Using pliers, close a calotte crimp over the knot.

Wooden Necklace from the Philippines

Woods from the Philippines which are used for beadmaking include the kamagong, bayong, gemelina, pangantuhan, and lambabaud. These woods are cut, polished, and waxed, producing beads of wonderfully rich colors marked with the grain of the wood.

Though you may not have access to genuine Philippine beads, similar wooden beads are available from other sources. This necklace is also attractive if you increase the length and omit the clasp; in this case, finish in the same way as the jet necklace project on page 29.

2 Thread the needle onto all 4 strands and add 4 wooden tubes and 1 round bead. Separate the strands and thread 32 tubes onto 1 strand only.

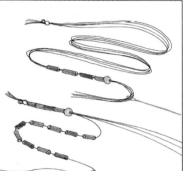

Materials

157 bayong tubes, ⅜ inch

2 round wooden or brown
    ceramic beads, ¼-inch
    diameter

5 yards thread

1 clip clasp and ring

2 calotte crimps

beading needle

needlenosed pliers

Total length:

    18 inches (shortest strand),

    22 inches (longest strand)

3 Thread the remaining 3 strands with 37, 39, and 41 tubes respectively. Rethread the needle onto all 4 strands and thread on 1 round bead and the last 4 wooden tubes.

Hint

Calotte crimps are the simplest way of finishing off a necklace neatly and securely. The tiny hinged cups clamp shut over a knot, and loops can then be attached to the clasp.

4 Tie an overhand knot as near to the last tube as possible and squeeze the other crimp shut over the knot. Attach the clip clasp to one crimp and the ring to the other, then neatly cut off the loose ends of thread.

Oceania

Oceania covers a wide variety of cultures, ranging from the Highlands of Papua New Guinea, where the people of one valley speak a language totally different from those in neighboring valleys, to the large, buzzing, cosmopolitan cities of Australia and New Zealand. Papua New Guinea is a nation in transition, but its tribal people wear spectacular beads, often of cowrie shells, as well as wonderful featherworked headdresses made from the plumage of the many species of Birds of Paradise. Their frequent ceremonial gatherings, known as "sing-sings", are always a fascinating experience for the visitor.

There have been beads, especially of shells, found in Australian aboriginal burial sites dating back thousands of years. Now, modern Australians make great use of all kinds of natural materials, ranging from beautiful opals to eucalyptus "gum nuts" and extraordinary Broome pearls.

Maori *tiki* figures from New Zealand are carved out of greenstone, which is a form of jade, while dark paua shells make beads of great beauty.

Shells and other marine objects are used to make beads all over Polynesia and the other island groups of the southwestern Pacific.

Above A Highlander from Papua New Guinea, wearing beads made from shells and natural materials.

Below A necklace of "gum nuts" made from the seed pods of various Australian eucalyptus trees. The painted dots and lines in the decoration is based on the traditional paintings of some Central Australian Aboriginal groups.

Above A woman at a traditional gathering in the Highlands of Papua New Guinea, wearing Bird of Paradise feathers and beads of cowries and other shells. Her red-and-white painted face shows she belongs to the Imbong'gu tribe.

Left A tribal necklace from Papua New Guinea which includes cuscus fur, seed and shell beads, as well as boars tusks. Boars have both ceremonial and social importance to the people.

Rarotonga Shell Necklaces

Long strands of shells to be worn as necklaces are a typical product of the Polynesian Islands. These small conus shells, which can be seen sprinkled liberally along almost every beach in the Pacific, are often found with a hole in the cone, making drilling unnecessary.

These beads were bought from a beach vendor in Rarotonga, one of the most idyllic of the many holiday islands in the South Pacific, easily reached from New Zealand or Australia. However, any small local shells can be used to create a similar effect. Here, four strands are doubled over and twisted casually together. The shells can be strung at random, or separated into pale and dark tones before stringing.

Larger shells, interspersed with either silver or rocaille beads, would make splendid earrings. We suggest that you adapt the project for Balinese silver earrings on page 120, using shells.

Materials

For each strand:	beading needle
approximately 180 shells	clear glue
2½ yards cotton or nylon thread	*Total length: approximately 2 yards*

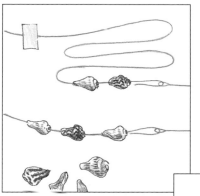

1 Either make a loose slip knot at one end of the thread, or tape it to the work surface while you thread on the shells.

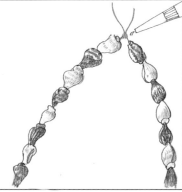

2 When you have reached the required length, tie the ends together in a secure overhand knot. Apply a small drop of glue and let it dry before cutting off the loose ends.

The Americas

The mysterious fable of El Dorado, the myth of the serpent god Quetzalcoatl, the gold of the Incas, the emeralds of Colombia, the jade of the Aztecs, the magic-lines of the Nazca—all are part of the rich history of the Americas. Flourishing beadmaking traditions were established by the Olmecs who, from 1200 B.C., became the great civilizers of Central America.

Olmec beadmakers in what is now Mexico worked in jadeite, the most important material in the region. A variety of jade, it ranges in color from almost white to nearly black, and it continued to be revered by the Aztecs.

Goldworking was of the highest importance to many South American cultures. Their religion was based on worship of the sun, so sunlight glinting on this bright and burnished metal had special significance.

With extraordinary skill they could make gold beads so tiny it is almost impossible to believe that they were made so long ago.

Left Brazilian coconut shell beads carved into the shapes of birds and fish.
Above Pre-Columbian gold warrior figure cast in lost-wax technique.

Left Native American in Arizona, wearing jocla strings (once worn as earrings) together with rough turquoise and heishi.
Right Kyapo man from the Brazilian Amazon wearing feathers and rocailles.
Previous pages From left: Peruvian hand-decorated ceramic bead necklace; Native American collar of bone, brass, and turquoise; necklace from Guatemala of European white heart trade beads strung with locally made metal pieces; necklace or turquoise and heishi beads from Arizona.

Other materials—less likely to survive than stone or metal—included shells, the iridescent wings of beetles, bone, teeth, claws, and feathers, which continue to be used by the indigenous peoples of the equatorial forests.

In North America, Native Americans made wampum beads, used both as currency and as a form of communication. Before European colonization, the tribes had used many bead materials, including pearls, claws, bone, porcupine quills, shells, and feathers. Later, they took colorful European rocaille trade beads and turned them into an art form, which is now one of the most recognizable forms of American beadwork.

New Mexican Silver Inlaid with Semiprecious Stones

New Mexican Navajo Silver

New Mexican Semiprecious Stone Animal Fetishes

Native American Wampum

Contemporary Foiled Glass by Alice Zimmerman, U.S.

Contemporary Foiled Glass by Susan Simons, U.S.

Kingman Mine Turquoise, Arizona

Contemporary Glass by Eric Mort, U.S.

Coated Plastic "Silver" and "Gold," New York

Mexican Onyx

Coated Plastic "Brass," U.S.

Contemporary Glass, U.S.

Mexican "Foam" Turquoise

Guatemalan Greenstone

Lucky Beans from Colombia and Guatemala

Job's Tears, Seeds from Brazil and Colombia

Ecuadoran Carved Vegetable Ivory

Ecuadoran "Gold" Glass

Peruvian Hand-decorated Glazed Ceramics

Peruvian Hand-decorated Ceramics

Peruvian Hand-decorated Glazed Ceramics

Peruvian Unglazed Ceramics

Map labels: BERING SEA · Los Angeles · CANADA · Ottawa · New York · U.S.A. · GRAND CANYON · Santo Domingo · Albuquerque · MEXICO · GULF OF MEXICO · Miami · CARIBBEAN SEA · GUATEMALA · BELIZE · HONDURAS · EL SALVADOR · NICARAGUA · COSTA RICA · PANAMA · COLOMBIA · VENEZUELA · GUYANA · SURINAM · FRENCH GUIANA · ECUADOR · PERU · BRAZIL · AMAZON · PACIFIC OCEAN · ATLANTIC OCEAN · Pisac · BOLIVIA · PARAGUAY · Rio de Janeiro · São Paulo · ARGENTINA · URUGUAY

Native Americans

Natural materials found abundantly all over the continent, were the traditional bead-making materials of the Native American tribes. Shells were of particular importance, both as adornment and as wampum, the latter of which was used as currency and a form of communication. Mother-of-pearl, abalone, olivella, and dentalium shells were made into beads, and freshwater pearls from the Mississippi as well as sea pearls have been found in archaeological digs. However, in the south, the Pueblo and Navajo peoples made jewelry with turquoise and later silver, producing a distinctive regional style.

When the Europeans arrived, in a story repeated over the entire continent, they avariciously plundered as much gold and silver as possible, giving in return glass beads, at first mostly from Venice, but later from Bohemia and Holland. Made in vast quantities, these

Above A fine early 1900s graduated turquoise necklace from New Mexico. Each bead was individually worked and carved.

Left A man from Canada's Blackfoot tribe wearing the fine beadwork for which Native Americans are well known. The two white disk beads were traditionally made from buffalo bone.

Right This legging, closely worked with seed beads or rocailles, is an excellent example of fine Native American beadwork.

Right A Cherokee woman from North Carolina making intricate beadwork using brightly colored rocailles. Rocailles were not used until after European colonization, but soon became a distinctive feature of Native American beadwork.

bright seed beads were put to good use by native artists and craftsmen, becoming a distinctive feature of their work. Buffalo hide saddlebags, moccasins, clothing, bonnets, and headdresses were stitched with the intricate geometric designs that are the most recognizable trademark of Native American workmanship. In particular, these seed beads were sewn onto skins in place of porcupine quills, which were much more difficult to work.

Many now highly collectable beads were traded in the early days. These included the Nueva Cadiz beads (so called because they were first rediscovered in Nueva Cadiz in Venezuela), Hudson Bay beads (also known as "white heart" or Cornaline d'Aleppo), Russian beads (the faceted Bohemian beads that arrived in North America with the fur trade

via the Russian route across the Bering Sea), and "pony" beads, the small glass beads introduced by the French and so called because they were transported by traders on ponies.

Wampum

When European settlers arrived, they found Native Americans using wampum shell beads. They considered them "Indian money," used as currency until the mid-eighteenth century. However, the tribes used them mainly as a means of communication, with information based on the order of arrangement.

Above Monument Valley, between Arizona and Utah. *Left* From top; Kiowa man from south of the Arkansas River, wearing a fine headdress with beads; man from a Plains tribe wearing a dentalium shell collar; the wife of a Kiowa chief at the Gallup gathering in Arizona, wearing beaded headband, necklaces, and earrings; Zuni chief in a spectacular beaded feather headdress at Gallup; Navajo man wearing a breastplate of hair pipes and beads, fastened with leather thongs. Such breastplates made of shell hair pipes were widely worn among the Plains tribes from the 1850s onward. From the 1880s, bone hair pipe beads became popular.

135

Woven into belts, wristbands, or strings, they were part of almost every important event in society, such as the declaration of war, the making of peace, and the signing of treaties, as well as more personal family events, such as the celebration of marriages.

Made from the quahog or hard clam *(Venus mercenaria)*, wampum are found in two colors, white and purple, each of different value, the larger purple worth twice as much as the white. Large purple clams were rarer, because clams were fished for food while their flesh was young, white, and tender. White beads were also made from conches and periwinkles.

White beads generally carried benign meanings such as peace and friendship, while purple signified hostile intention such as the declaration of war. Wampum were woven into belts or similar objects, threaded onto thongs of leather or fiber. First used in the northeast, most famously by the Iroquois, they spread south to the Gulf of Mexico and west to the Dakotas.

Wampum were first ground down on stones, then holes drilled with a nail stuck into a cane or reed. This was rolled against the thigh with one hand, while the shell was held in the other.

European settlers began using wampum as money, producing it with more advanced drilling techniques. As a result, the market was soon flooded, and wampum was abandoned in favor of silver coins. But the prestige of the beads survived, and they continued to be made for their original purpose until late in the nineteenth century, as the beautiful examples seen in museums today bear witness. The Iroquois League is working toward having those examples returned to their people.

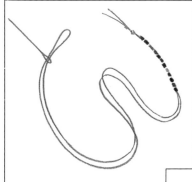

1 Lay out the fetishes in a symbolic or attractive sequence, with the turtle in the center. Double the thread, attach the needle to one end, and tie 3 or 4 overhand knots in the other end. Thread on an inch of heishi.

Zuni Animal Fetish Necklace

Native Americans, particularly noted for their silver and turquoise work, also made small animal motifs, known as fetishes, using jasper, mother-of-pearl, and soapstone as well as turquoise. This simple but evocative necklace was bought from Native American traders in a Santa Fe market. The turtle symbolizes mother earth, the frog, tadpole, and waterbirds symbolize water, while the horse, rabbit, dog, fox, buffalo, fish, and birds are animals seen every day. Collect your own fetishes to create a personal symbolism or make a story in a sequence that has meaning for you.

2 (Right) Start threading on the fetishes, leaving enough space between them to allow them to lie well when you are wearing the necklace; these are spaced at about ½ inch intervals, with 1 inch on either side of the turtle.

2 (Continued) When you have finished stringing, make 3 or 4 overhand knots as close to the final bead as possible.

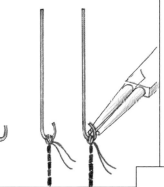

3 (Left) To attach the conical necklet ends, use pliers to form an open loop in one piece of wire. Hook it securely through the knots at one end of the necklace and then close the loop with pliers. Apply a dab of glue to the knots and allow it to dry before cutting off the ends.

Materials

20 stone animal fetishes

1 turquoise turtle (optional)

28-inch string of turquoise
   and shell heishi
   (small, uniform beads)

2 conical silver necklet
   ends

1 silver figure-eight
   ring and hook

2 yards thread

1 beading needle or
   fine-wire needle

2½ inches of 0.8 mm wire,
   cut in half

round-nosed pliers

clear glue

Total length: 28 inches

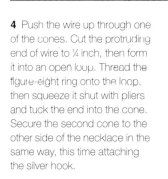

4 Push the wire up through one of the cones. Cut the protruding end of wire to ¼ inch, then form it into an open loop. Thread the figure-eight ring onto the loop, then squeeze it shut with pliers and tuck the end into the cone. Secure the second cone to the other side of the necklace in the same way, this time attaching the silver hook.

The Pueblo People of Santo Domingo

Santo Domingo in Arizona was destroyed by its inhabitants in 1692 in an attempt to resist domination by the Spanish. The town was rebuilt in 1700, and since then its people have attempted to continue their way of life as it was then.

Although almost all of the craftspeople who work in Santo Domingo resort to the modern convenience of electric polishing machines and drills, there are still some traditional craftsmen who eschew modernity and continue to use the hand pump drill as their ancestors have always done. In fact, beads found in the Anasazi burials from the Pueblo Cultures of A.D. 827–1200 at Chaco Canyon are very like the beads being produced today.

These techniques, though simple, require both enormous skill and a great of patience. Interestingly, these same processes have been developed and used the world over by many different cultures and at different times.

To produce a turquoise bead, a piece of rough stone is gradually ground down with sand, using water as a lubricant, producing a disk shape—a process taking the best part of 1½ hours. A further half-hour's work on a pump drill is needed to grind the hole.

The flat beads are strung onto a thin metal wire, then polished and smoothed on various flat stones to produce a perfect string of disks. A final polish with deer hide brings out the sheen, and a handmade clasp will complete a necklace that could easily have been made many centuries before. Even the fact that stones and shells are now likely to have been imported echoes the great trading routes that wound their way across North America as early as 6000 B.C.

Left The Rio Grande near Santo Domingo Pueblo, west of Santa Fe in New Mexico.

Above Heishi beads made of shell from the Pacific, which were traded into New Mexico.

Left A fine necklace of greenish turquoise stones and heishi beads, and a choker of heishi beads and bluish turquoise from the Kingman mine in western Arizona.

Right This fine necklace and earrings of turquoise and shell heishi beads is typical of the craftsmanship found among the bead-makers of New Mexico's Zuni people

Above Craftspeople of Santo Domingo with stalls in the Governor's Square Market, Santa Fe. They take turns at having a stall, and sell their work to customers from all over the world. Only jewelry hand-made by this community can be sold here, and the entry requirements are strictly enforced.

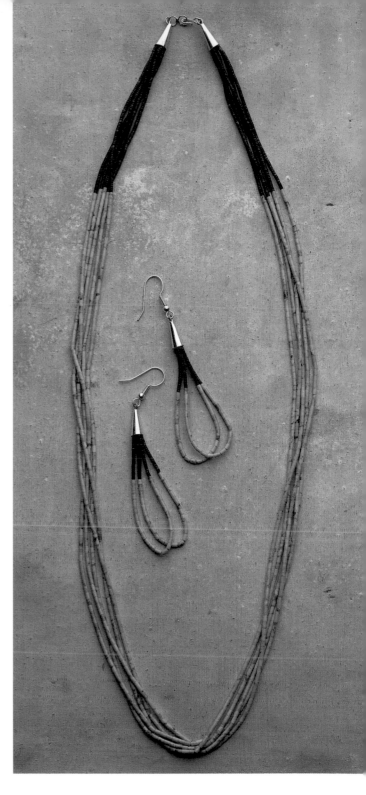

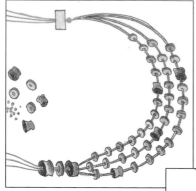

1 Join the 3 lengths of thread with an overhand knot 200 mm from one end; tape to the work surface. Thread 350 mm of each strand with heishi, large turquoise disks, and coral chunks. Ensure that the strands lie well together, then thread the ends through the central coral and turquoise beads.

Heishi, Turquoise, and Coral Necklace

The small, regularly shaped shell beads in this necklace are called heishi. Strings of heishi can be found in a variety of colors and materials, and are widely available in Santo Domingo and across the Southwest. The looped tassels are like the traditional Navajo *jocla* ear decorations, sometimes incorporated in necklaces.

These heishi were probably not handmade, the coral would have been imported, and since native turquoise is now quite rare, the turquoise is probably Chinese. However, the design and its wrapped thread closure are traditional.

2 (Right) Separate 1 strand and thread on 1 coral bead, 3 inches of small turquoise disks, 3 coral beads, 3 inches turquoise, and another coral bead. Bring the other 2 strands together and thread the doubled strand with the same sequence of beads.

Materials

73 turquoise disks,
⅜ inch diameter

11 coral chunks

16-inch strand turquoise
disks, ⅜ inch diameter

10 coral beads, ⅜ inch
diameter

5 strings heishi, 16 inches
each

4 yards polycotton or spun
nylon thread, cut into 3
equal lengths

9 yards soft cotton thread

beading needle

sewing needle

masking tape

*Total length: 33 inches, plus
the 5-inch tassel*

3 (Above) Bring the 3 strands together again and thread them back up through the 3 central beads. Thread the 3 strands that make up the other side of the necklace until they measure the same as the first side.

4 (Below left) Remove the needle and join the 3 strands with an overhand knot as close to the last beads as possible. Trim the excess thread to 8 inches to match the other side. Twist each side of the necklace loosely, then join the 2 sides by curling the loose ends over each other, tying them together temporarily.

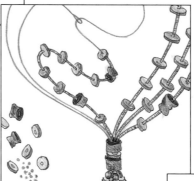

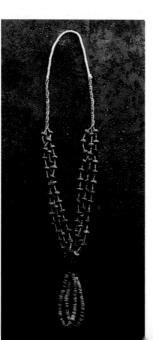

5 (Far right) Lay one end of the cotton thread 2 inches down the unbeaded ends, hold it in place, and begin winding around the threads from just above the final beads. When you reach the beads on the other side, thread a sewing needle and knot the thread onto itself, then push it into the center of the whipping before you cut off the end.

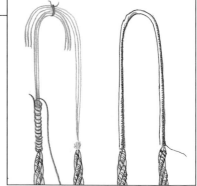

Mexico: Jade, Gold, and Modern Glass

Bead traditions in Central America date back more than 9,500 years, but beads are found in greatest numbers in archaeological sites from about 1,500 B.C. Beads made of elaborately carved jade or gold indicated wealth and status in Mayan society. Jade, imported from what is now Guatemala, was regarded even more highly than gold, and its colors ranged from the subtle grays and blue-greens so much admired by the Olmecs to the leaf and emerald greens preferred by the Maya.

Modern production methods mean that some of the old skills have been forgotten, but Mexican beadmakers still work in materials ranging from natural stones such as onyx, to shell, coral, seeds, clay, local amber, and the ever-important silver. Plastic and glass beads are made depicting chiles, fruit, vegetables, fish, birds, and copies of Pre-Columbian gold figurines.

The Huichol People
Glass beads appeared in Central America after the Spanish invasions and found their way to the most remote areas. Even the Huichol, from

Above Jadeite or greenstone beads of the type found in Mayan graves, probably mined in Guatemala near the Negro River. It is not as brightly colored as Burmese jade.

Below left From the time of the Spanish conquistadores, Mexico received trade beads from Europe, such as the white heart, red glass, yellow bicones, and Venetian glass beads in this necklace. The little metal *milagro* ("miracle") legs, or health fetishes, were locally made.

Right Three necklaces of banded Mexican onyx, one clearly showing the knotting method used in stringing.

Top right From top: Kena Bautista de la Rosa is the daughter of a famous Huichol artisan, Francisco Bautista Carillo. She uses a fine beading needle to decorate a bowl with rocailles applied onto a fine layer of beeswax, and pine pitch. She uses symbols linked to the spiritual beliefs of the Huichol people.

Right Huichol mask of brightly colored rocailles. Religious traditions maintain that the more colorful the pattern, the more the wearer will be noticed by the gods.

a remote area of northern Mexico, have been affected. They are deeply spiritual, and religion permeates every part of their lives, including their decorative and bead designs showing gods, sacred plants, and animals. These symbols are used to decorate clothing, necklaces, and earrings, using a profusion of the brightly colored glass rocailles of which they are particularly fond. This elaborate beadwork echoes their long tradition of textile weaving: before they had access to beads they made bright yarn paintings, where vibrantly colored wools were pressed onto boards coated with beeswax. Now beads are not only embroidered onto textiles but may also be embedded into beeswax applied to gourds or similar items.

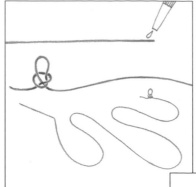

1 Lay out the beads to determine the stringing sequence, starting with 2 peridot bicones, placing the coins at equal intervals and matching the beads on both sides of the cross. Stiffen about 1½ inches of one end of the thread with glue, allow it to dry, then tie a temporary slip knot 3 inches from the other end.

Necklace of "Peridots" from Guatemala

Guatemala is largely populated by Indians descended from Mayans who lived there before the Spanish arrived in 1523. Traditional Indian rites are still practiced in tandem with Catholic ceremonies. This necklace, bought in a market in the 1970s, is made of red glass beads, glass bicones cut to look like peridots, coins, and a cross. Peridots are regarded as protection against the Evil Eye and diseases of the liver. In ancient times, the main source was the Red Sea island of Topazios (St. John's Island), which led to the mineral erroneously being named topaz.

2 String the first half of the necklace, threading on the beads in the planned sequence.

3 If the cross has a loop attached, thread it directly onto the main strand. If it has a hole drilled through the top, tie it with a short length of thread and a strong knot onto the central point of the main strand. Thread on the remaining beads and coins to match the pattern on the first side of the necklace, finishing with 2 peridot bicones.

Hint
Beads of semiprecious stones such as peridots can be quite expensive. However, you can sometimes be lucky and find them in tangled, broken strings in flea markets or junk shops, Otherwise, you could substitute glass beads in a similar color.

Materials

68–69 peridot bicones,
  ¼–½ inches

30 red glass beads,
  ¼ inch diameter

6 coins, side-drilled

1 metal cross, 2½ inches

2 yards strong twisted
  thread

clear glue

*Total length excluding
  cross: 27 inches*

4 Undo the temporary slip knot and join both sides of the necklace together with 2 firm overhand knots as close to the last beads as possible. Apply a drop of glue to secure the knot and let it dry before cutting off the ends.

Beads in Peru: Past and Present

Peru has been the cradle of many great Pre-Columbian civilizations, including the Chavin, Moche, Chimu, and Inca. (The Incas, in spite of their fame, flourished for only about a hundred years before they were overwhelmed by the Spanish.) Each civilization left behind a wealth of exquisitely wrought handwork.

The Pre-Columbian Past

The Chavin civilization flourished in Peru from 1250–300 B.C. and splendid sculpture and architecture survives from that era. Gold beads of hammered sheet metal were found in tombs from the Moche era, and gold continued to be important in the later Chimu and Inca cultures.

Superbly crafted ornaments excavated from tombs include beads of gold, turquoise, rock crystal, lapis lazuli, jasper, cornelian, and shell. Tiny turquoise beads as small as ¹⁄₁₆ inch in diameter have been found perfectly drilled through, as well as copper beads which have oxidized, but still show their shape.

Above and left Ceramic beads made in the village of Pisac from the same clay deposits used by the Incas. *Above right* Decorating a small ceramic bead with designs inspired by the landscape, llamas, and birds. All Peruvian beads are hand-decorated.

Organic materials generally do not survive the centuries very well, except in extraordinary climatic conditions such as the bogs of Scandinavia, the deserts of Egypt, and the arid altitudes of the Andes. Those objects that have survived in Peru include wood, feathers, animal teeth and claws, bones, shells, and seeds. Feathers were highly prized throughout the region, traded then, as now, from their areas of origin, including the Amazonian basin and the lowland jungles.

Superbly worked Inca gold hardly survives even in museums. The Spanish invaders, greedily gathering up all the gold they could find, melted it down, ignoring the fine craftsmanship they were destroying. The proceeds were divided between the invaders and the Spanish king, who demanded one-fifth of all booty.

However ancient ceramic vessels and beads

have been found and these traditions still continue. All the way from Peru to Mexico, the typical twisted multiple-strand terra-cotta bead necklace designs worn by the Pre-Columbian peoples continue to be worn today.

Beadmakers of Pisac

Centered around the city of Cuzco, ancient capital of the Incas, and in the town of Pisac, where there are also Inca ruins, the tradition of ceramic beadmaking thrives, incorporating

Above The small village of Pisac, southwest of Machu Picchu, lies in mountainous terrain close to the Urubamba River valley, high in the Andes.

Right From top: Beads are decorated in workshops off these lanes in Pisac; this potter prepares ceramic beads to be fired in her outdoor kiln; the beads, in various typical sizes and shapes, are fired in these attractive clay vessels; each bead, held on a long pin, is hand-decorated with circles, while horizontal lines are formed by holding the brush against the bead and spinning the bead around the pin.

many of the decorative motifs of that earlier civilization. Village artisans and larger enterprises alike form part of a ceramic industry that stretches even as far as the capital, Lima. Production is flourishing, due partly to the great popularity of these beads in Europe and North America—and Peruvian beads are even being copied in the Far East, especially in the Philippines, for sale around the world.

The delicate Peruvian beads are instantly recognizable, with their skillfully handpainted designs of cacti, llamas, mythical birds, and traditional geometric shapes, in colors ranging from bold and eyecatching to subtle and earthy. The peoples reared in the Inca tradition produce designs that are true representations of their culture for, although Roman Catholicism is practiced here, the current of the ancient beliefs runs just under the surface.

Pisac nestles in the Urubamba River valley near Cuzco, and high above lies the famous ruined city of Machu Picchu. In Pisac, bead-making is a traditional family business. The clay comes from the valley, and once cleansed of impurities, it is fashioned into traditional shapes. It is expertly rolled around a needle to form *lagrimas* (teardrops), then a small hand-tool is used to squeeze the clay into long tubes like spaghetti, which is then cut into short lengths by hand.

Larger enterprises now have electric kilns, but artisans still use the traditional open-air kilns. After firing, these are unstacked, and the cooled beads are taken to the painting workshops, where children often work after school. The painted beads are glazed and then fired a second time.

1 Lay out the beads in a pleasing order. Make a temporary slip knot at one end of the leather strand and thread on the beads. Hold up the necklace by the ends of the leather so that the beads hang in the center, then make an overhand knot above the last bead on each side.

2 To make an adjustable knot, arrange both ends of the leather so that they overlap each other by about an inch. Tie the right-hand end in an overhand knot to the main left-hand strand, then tie the left-hand end to the main right-hand strand in the same way.

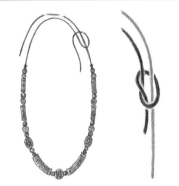

Peru Clay Necklace

These simple Peruvian beads have a natural ethnic quality. The various shapes and different earthy tones of the beads complement each other, and those in the earrings are highlighted with silver beads. You could also substitute the brightly painted clay beads decorated with typical Peruvian designs of cacti, llamas, birds and traditional geometrical shapes. The necklace is made by threading beads onto a thin leather strand. If you use the adjustable knot method, you can slip the necklace over your head and then shorten it to your chosen length.

The carved clay beads for this necklace were bought in a bead shop in England, but you can choose any shapes and colors that appeal to you or that you might find in your travels.

Materials

Necklace	Earrings
4 carved clay tubes, ⅞ inch	2 carved clay tubes, ⅞ inch
2 curved clay tubes, 1¾ inches	2 carved clay cylinders, ½ inch
1 carved clay cylinder, ½ inch	2 clay rounds, ⅜ inch diameter
2 carved clay ovals, ¾ inch	8 silver disks, ¼ inch diameter
8 clay rounds, ⅜ inch diameter	4 silver round beads, ⅛ inch diameter
4 carved clay rounds, ⅜ inch diameter	2 silver ear-hooks
8 dark clay rounds, ¼ inch diameter	2 silver headpins, 2¾ inches
38 inches leather, ¹⁄₁₆ inch thick	tweezers or round-nosed pliers
Total length: 35 inches	wire cutters

Peru Clay Earrings

1 To make the earrings, thread a small silver bead onto the headpin, followed by the other beads in your chosen order, ending with a small silver bead. Cut the pin to leave a length of ¼ inch. Using tweezers or pliers, grasp the pin just above the last bead and bend it back to form a right angle. Grasping the end of the pin, turn it to form a loop. Slide the ring of the ear-hook onto it before squeezing it shut.

149

Pre-Columbian Cultures

Before 1492, when Columbus made landfall in the New World, thriving civilizations had been in existence for some 2,500 years, comparable to the ancient Egyptians and the Romans. Those civilizations are known as Pre-Columbian (before Columbus), not to be confused with the modern state of Colombia.

So who were they, what can we learn from their architectural and artistic legacies, and especially what kind of beads have survived from those 25 centuries? The Mexican Olmec, Maya, Aztec, and Toltec cultures, the Chavin, Moche, Nazca, Tiwanaku, and Inca civilizations from the Andes, the Tairona, and Sinu

of Colombia produced images of gods, jade figurines, turquoise masks, gold, and jewels—all fueling the avarice of Spanish conquistadores in the service of a king greedy for gold to fund his costly wars in Europe.

The beads that have survived from these cultures are generally of natural materials. Shells, rock crystal, mother of pearl, and agates are the predominant materials, since the seeds and organic materials they may have used have rotted away. There was also a flourishing metal-working industry, in particular in Colombia where lost-wax gold casting was brought to an extraordinarily high standard. Splendid gold ornaments of warriors, owls, frogs, figures, animals, and masks in a vast collection of pendants, pectorals, ear ornaments, votive figurines, plus simple beads and spacers with fluid and abstract shapes have been uncovered to bear testament to their skill.

Above One of the great Pre-Columbian sites—Inca ruins, Machu Picchu, Peru.
Above right Ruins of Mayan temple, Palenque, Mexico.
Center, right Colombian Pre-Columbian bow-drilled stone and shell beads.
Opposite Pre-Columbian cornelian necklace.

1 First make the hanging strands and plan the sequence in which you will add them to the main strand. Cut 43 pieces of thread, 14 inches long. For the simpler strands, knot a piece of thread at one end and thread a beading needle onto the other. Thread 6 inches of beads, seeds, and nuts—if they do not have holes already, push a thick

Colombian Seed and Feather Necklace

B rightly bedecked with feathers and seeds, this ceremonial necklace from the Vaupés, a tributary of the Amazon, is a joyful mix of natural materials and imported glass beads in the tradition of the Pre-Columbian Tairona culture of Colombia and Venezuela. Besides being superb goldsmiths, they used found objects in their crafts, such as bright feathers, pods, seeds (to ensure a good crop), nuts, teeth, coins, shells, and glass rocailles. If Colombian materials are not available to you, use your own local materials to create a personal version of this flamboyant necklace.

needle through the center of each. Thread the needle around the last bead and back through the next 2 beads, leaving a loop large enough to thread a needle through for attaching the hanging strand to the main thread. Knot the end securely around the strand, apply a drop of glue, and allow it to dry before cutting off the loose end.

2 For a feathered end-piece, first drill a hole in the top of a half seed or shell. Bind the feathers together with thread, then push the bound ends into the shell and glue them in position.
For a looped end-piece, cut a length of thread 17 inches long, knot one end, and thread on 6 inches of beads and seeds. Thread on a coin and another ¾

inch of beads, then thread the needle back through the strand ¾ inch from the coin. Finish with a loop as before.
For more elaborate strands, first tie a tooth, coin, large seed (whole or cut in half), or feathered end-piece onto one end of the thread, then thread 6 inches of beads and seeds, finishing with a loop as before.

3 Cut a piece of thread 43 inches long for the main strand. Tie a temporary knot 2¼ inches from one end and thread a needle onto the other end. Thread 32 inches of seeds. Lay out the hanging strands in the planned sequence, then thread them onto the main strand, interspersing each with a large seed.

4 When all the strands are attached, make sure that they hang well, then thread another 32 inches of seeds. Undo the temporary knot and tie both sides together with 2 secure knots. Apply a drop of glue and let it dry before cutting off the loose ends.

Materials

about 100 seeds, ½ inch

about 250 seeds, ¼ inch

about 400 large rocailles

assorted nuts, seeds, teeth, feathers, shells, drilled coins, and glass beads

19 yards strong, fine thread

beading needle

tapestry needle

hand drill, with a 1/32 inch bit

Total length excluding

hanging strands:

28 inches; 43 strands of

approximately 6 inches

Brazil: Stones, Seeds, and Feathers

Semiprecious stones are found in many sites around the world, especially in the very old shield areas of all continents.

Brazil is one of the major regions where a vast variety of gemstones occurs. Amethyst, agate, aquamarine, alexandrite, citrine, garnet, diamonds, hematite, opal, rock crystal, zircon, rose quartz, tourmaline, and others are mined then distributed as raw material all around the world to stonecutting centers such as Idar-Oberstein in Germany, and in the Far East, where they are converted into beads, carvings, and objets d'art.

In the state of Minas Gerais, there are many minerological museums and reminders of past mining history. In the same area is the town of Teôfilo Otôni, the site of a great market for crystals and semiprecious stones. The stones are shipped on to the important beadmaking centers, such as Idar-Oberstein in Germany, or

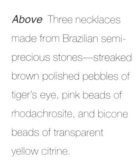

Above Three necklaces made from Brazilian semiprecious stones—streaked brown polished pebbles of tiger's eye, pink beads of rhodachrosite, and bicone beads of transparent yellow citrine.

Below left Brazil is the source of many semiprecious stones used in beadmaking around the world. Clockwise from far left are amazonite, rose quartz, leopardskin poppy jasper, and amethyst. Stonecutting industries in Europe and the Far East depleted their own deposits of such stones, and mines in South America now supply these industries with high-quality stones.

to China and Japan. Stonecutting industries grew up in these centers based on local deposits of semiprecious stones, but over the centuries the mines have been worked out and supplies had to be acquired from elsewhere.

Indigenous Peoples

Much of Brazil forms the catchment area for the Amazon, which is one of the world's largest surviving areas of rainforest. The tribes of the Amazon Basin, especially the Kyapo and the Yanomami, are well known to anthropologists and Western media as a result of their efforts to protect their lands from the encroachment of logging companies.

The Kyapo live in the south of the Amazon Basin and have an interesting bead tradition, using seeds, stones, feathers, and shells. Rock crystal is worn by male elders, while feathers indicate the age, clan, and status of the wearer. Other Amazonian tribes also use seeds and feathers in belts, necklaces, and headdresses, the featherwork of the Urubu-Kaapor tribe being particularly fine. Various nuts and seeds are used, including "vegetable ivory" (which can be carved like real ivory), Job's tears or nickernuts (thought to bring good luck and ward off the devil), the poisonous "snake eye" seeds, the red and black seeds of the "necklace tree" (*Ormosia monosperma*), and the rosary bean.

Among the Kyapo, lipplugs and ear ornaments are seen as linked to intelligence and understanding. The size of a lip plug indicates the wearer's skills as an orator, and the wearing of ear ornaments is a sign of human intelligence in the ability to understand speech. Babies' ear-lobes are pierced and stone plugs inserted in the belief that this will give them the ability to hear and to understand speech— the plugs are then replaced by strings of beads when the child does eventually learn to speak.

Museums

Many museums have interesting bead collections. This list is just the tip of the iceberg and we would be delighted to hear from readers who may have discovered other interesting museums with bead collections.

United Kingdom
Pitt Rivers Museum, Oxford
Museum of Archaeology
    and Anthropology
    Cambridge University
Museum of Mankind,
    London
British Museum, London
Natural History Museum,
    London (stones and rocks)
Hornimann Museum,
    London
Jet Museum
    Whitby, Yorkshire

France
Musée de l'Homme*, Paris
Musée de la Mosaique
    et des Emaux, Briare
Musée Municipal de Nevers
    (glassmaking)

Denmark
Amber Museum, Copenhagen

Germany
Linden-Museum,* Stuttgart
Staaliches Museum für
    Völkerkunde, Stuttgart
Museum für Völkerkunde*,
    Berlin
Museum of Idar-Oberstein

Netherlands
Afrika Museum*,
    Nijmegen, Gelderland
Tropenmuseum*, Amsterdam

Poland
Amber Museum, Malbork

Czech Republic
Museum of Glass, Jablonec
National Museum, Prague

Italy
Museo Vetraio, Murano, Venice
Museo Livarino,
    Torre del Greco, near Naples
Cameos & Corals Factory,
    Ravello

Switzerland
Barbier-Mueller Museum,
    Geneva

Kenya
Kenya Museums, Nairobi

Morocco
Palais de Bahia Museum,
    Marrakesh (many jewelry
    artifacts, including beads)

USA
Prescott Bead Museum,
    Prescott, Arizona
Zach-Low Turquoise Museum,
    Albuqerque, New Mexico
Metropolitan Museum of Art,
    New York
Museum of New Mexico,
    Santa Fe, Arizona
The Picard College,
    Carmel, California
Mungei Museum,
    San Diego, California

Canada
Royal Ontario Museum
    Toronto

* Denotes special African interest.

Bead Suppliers

USA

Beadbox Inc.
P.O. Box 6035
Scottsdale, AZ 85258

Beads Galore
2123 S. Priest Dr., #201
Tempe, AZ 85282

Beadworks
139 Washington St.,
South Norwalk, CT 06854

Bourget Bros.
1636 11th Street
Santa Monica, CA 90404

Fire Mountain Gems
28195 Redwood Highway
Cave Junction,
OR 97523-9304

Garden of Beading
P.O. Box 1535
Redway, CA 95560

Rings & Things
P.O. Box 450
Spokane, WA 99210

Shipwreck Beads
2727 Westmoor Court SW
Olympia,
WA 98502-5754

Informational Resources:

The Austin Bead Society
P.O. Box 656
Austin, TX 78767–0656

The Bead Directory
P.O. Box 10103
Oakland, CA 94610

The Bead Fairies Page
http://www.mcs.net/-simone/beadfairies.html
Specializes in web links to bead sites and information on beading techniques, books, patterns, and tips.

The Bead Society of Orange County
An Affiliate of The Bowers Museum of Cultural Art
2002 N Main St.
Santa Ana, CA 92706

The Center for the Study of Beadwork
P.O. Box 13719
Portland, OR 97213

The Sierra Bead Society
13878 Lear Blvd.
Stead, NV 89506

The Society of Bead Researchers
P.O. Box 7304
Eugene, OR 97401

CANADA

Beads and Plenty More
Ste 113-755 N,. Calgary,
Alberta T2J 0N3

Pacific Western Crafts
Box 40024,
Victoria,
British Columbia, U8W 3N3

Bead Box
1234 Robson Street
Vancouver,
British Columbia, B6E 1C1

Photography Acknowledgments

The publisher thanks the photographers and organizations for their kind permission to reproduce the following photographs in this book:

2–3 Richard Foster; 13 above right Impact/Ben Edwards; 14 above right and below Janet Coles; 16 center and below Janet Coles; 20 left Robert Estall Photo Agency/Fabby Nielsen; 20 right Robert Budwig; 22 above Janet Coles; 24 left Andes Press Agency/ Carlos Reyes-Manzo; 26 above left Janet Coles; 31 left Janet Coles; 34 below Museum Idar-Oberstein; 38 left and center ffotograff/Patricia Aithie; 43 below left Hemisphères/Bruno Barbier; 43 below right Robert Estall Photo Library/Angela Fisher; 44 left Trip/Trip; 44 center and right Robert Estall Photo Agency/Angela Fisher; 45 below Robert Budwig; 50 Hutchison Library/Charlie Nairn; 52 above right Graham Harrison (courtesy British Museum); 52 below right Tropix/M Fleetwood; 54 Richard Foster; 56 below right Robert Estall Photo Agency/ Angela Fisher; 57 left Robert Estall Photo Agency/Carol Beckwith; 60 above left Panos/Liba Taylor; 60 below left Hutchison Library; 60 below right Trip/D Saunders; 61 Richard Foster; 65 above left Impact/James Barlow; 65 below left Zefa; 66 left Trip/ J & F Teede; 69 above Robert Estall Photo Library/Angela Fisher; 70 left Robert Estall Photo Agency/Angela Fisher/Carol Beckwith; 71 top, above, center, below and bottom Robert Budwig; 73 left Robert Estall Photo Agency/Angela Fisher; 77 above Robert Harding Picture Library; 77 below left Robert Harding Picture Library; 77 below right Stephanie Colasanti; 78 below Janet Coles; 79 center Janet Coles; 80 Graham Harrison; 82 Janet Coles; 83 Trip/H Rogers; 90 left Robert Budwig; 90 above center Janet Coles; 91 left Hémispheres/Bertrand Cardel; 91 center Janet Coles; 92 center ffotograff/Nick Tapsell; 92 below Trip/ J Batten; 93 above left Impact/Christophe Bluntzer; 96 above Robert Budwig; 96 below right Robert Harding Picture Library/Ross Greetham; 103 below left Trip/Eric Smith; 104 above right Robert O'Dea; 110 above Michael Freeman; 114 center Trip/A Tory; 115 above right Janet Coles; 118 above right Panos Pictures/Guy Mansfield; 118 center left Tony Stone Images/Denis Waugh; 118 below Robert Budwig; 119 right Robert Budwig; 122 above Amanda Coles; 122 center Trip/ D Maybury; 122 below left Getty Images/David Hanson; 123 below Amanda Coles; 124 center left Andes Press Agency/Carlos Reyes-Manzo; 124 below Janet Coles; 128 above left Getty Images/ Christopher Arnesen; 128 above right Trip/E Smith; 132 below left Robert Harding Picture Library/Adam Woolfitt; 132 below right Thomas L Kelly; 134 above right Hutchison Library/ Robert Francis; 134 below left Trip/Eric Smith; 135 main picture and bottom Hemisphères/Patrick Frilet; 135 top Robert Harding Picture Library/Silvestris; 135 above Andes Press Agency/Carlos Reyes-Manzo; 135 center Robert Harding Picture Library/Paolo Koch; 135 below Robert Harding Picture Library/Adam Woolfitt; 138 below Robert Budwig; 139 left Robert Budwig; 143 Robert Budwig; 146 right Robert Budwig; 147 main picture, above, below and bottom Robert Budwig; 147 top Trip/M Barlow; 150 left and above right Hemisphères/ Betrand Gardel; 155 below right Thomas Kelly.

Special Photography by Jonathan Lovekin: Endpapers, 1, 4–11, 12, 13 center and below, 14 above center, 15, 16 above, 17–18, 20 center, 21, 22 below, 22–23, 24 center and right, 25, 26 below left and right, 27–30, 31 right, 33, 34 above, 35–37, 38 right, 39–42, 43 above, 45 above, 47–49, 51, 52 above center and below left, 53, 56 left, 57 right, 58–59, 60 above right, 62–64, 65 right, 66 center and right, 67–68, 69 below, 70 right, 71 main picture, 72, 73 right, 74–76, 78 above, 79 far left and right, 80–81, 82–83, 85–88, 90 below, 91 right, 92 above, 93 below left and right; 94–95; 96 left, 97–102, 103 center and right, 104 above left and below, 105–109, 110 below, 111–112, 114 left and right, 115 left and below, 116–117, 118 above left, 119 left, 120–121, 122 above, 122 below right, 123 above, 124 above, 124–5, 126–127, 128 below, 129–131, 132 above and center, 133, 134 above left and below right, 136–137, 138 above, 138–139, 139 right, 140–141, 142 143, 146 left and center, 148–9, 150 center and below right, 151–154, 155 left and above right, 156–160.

Jacket
Front jacket, Jonathan Lovekin; back jacket above left and right, below left and right, Jonathan Lovekin; above center Trip/Robert Belbin; center left Trip/Eric Smith; center right Hemisphère/ Christophe Boisvieux; below center Panos/Liba Taylor

Index

Acknowledgments

This book would not have been possible without the help of those who lent us pieces from their private collections and shared information invaluable in our research.

Special thanks to Joss and Alex May, Donald Simmonds, Amanda Coles, Lesley Schiff at the Talisman Gallery, Mel Watson, Peter Adler, Angela Fisher, Maria Alexander, Omar Mason at the Turkmen Gallery, Joss Graham at Oriental Textiles Gallery, Victor Lamont, Ruth Puddy, Bryan and Susi Reeves, Madeline Fenton, George Bristow, Annie Marshall, Jürgen Busch, Susan Wainwright, Peter Baumgarten, Jim Mellon, Marie Laure Aris, Jo Bonrosto, Pedro Sepulveda, Poem van Landewijk and Kingsley Safo in Ghana, Giorgio Filocamo, Giuliano and Gianni Moretti, Paolo Darin, Marie-Francoise Delaroziere, Patricia Woram and Troels Kloredal. In the USA to Herbert and Stephanie Budwig, Nancy Henrikson, Susan and Ann Geisert, Susan Simons, Nina Cooper, Bernie Lawitz at Beads Galore, Diana Pardue at the Heard Museum, Phoenix, and Gabrielle Liese at the Bead Museum, Prescott. To Hannah Terry for her beading expertise, and, in Europe, to modern bead designers Catherine Mannheim, Heather Bellman, Patrick Stern, and Angela Bielenberg, and the USA to Lucy Berganini and Karen Ovington. Finally to our publishers including Mark Latter and Zia Mattocks, and to Larraine Shamwana, Cathy Ebbels, Elsa Petersen-Schepelern, Jacqui Small, and Anne Ryland, who also lent us items from their collections.